NOMADS
The Memoir of a Southern Cameroonian

Emmanuel Fru Doh

Langaa Research & Publishing CIG
Mankon, Bamenda

Publisher:
Langaa RPCIG
Langaa Research & Publishing Common Initiative Group
P.O. Box 902 Mankon
Bamenda
North West Region
Cameroon
Langaagrp@gmail.com
www.langaa-rpcig.net

Distributed in and outside N. America by African Books Collective
orders@africanbookscollective.com
www.africanbookcollective.com

ISBN: 9956-790-89-3

© Emmanuel Fru Doh 2013

DISCLAIMER
All views expressed in this publication are those of the author and do not necessarily reflect the views of Langaa RPCIG.

Dedication

To the memory of Professor Linus Tongwo Asong,
an invaluable friend and colleague
who contradicted virtually every Cameroonian stereotype;
the true example of a Southern Cameroonian,
who was at home in Buea or in Bamenda
and served and entertained caring less
about these roots. He refused to succumb
to these artificial boundaries today imposed
on his people by unpatriotic kleptocrats
masquerading as leaders of the hour.

and

To all peace-loving Cameroonians,
especially to this side of the Mungo,
that you may always remember.

To God Almighty be Praise and Glory

Note

I changed my uncle's name in order to maintain his privacy and integrity. This venture is not about him, yet that is what it will become, I suspect, should I disclose his identity.

It is also worthwhile noting that from "Southern Cameroons," we have the terminology "Southern Cameroonians," which is used interchangeably with "West Cameroonians" and "Anglophone-Cameroonians" depending on the situation and time in history. This also applies to "La République du Cameroun" with "East Cameroonians" and "Francophones."

1

In life, it is mainly events that get people thinking and questioning about virtually everything, especially their identity, and so they look back to see where they are coming from in order to understand the present and so try to fathom what the future holds for them. In the land of my birth, those of us once referred to as Southern Cameroonians, and later West Cameroonians, have had just too many things visited upon us as a result of our reunification with La République du Cameroun for us to forget that easily. A few examples are the closing of the Bota oil mill, which produced and exported palm kernel oil; the engineered fall of Powercam and the deliberate transformation of the Yoke dam into ruins—Powercam was the corporation that used Yoke dam to supply West Cameroon with affordable electricity; the shutting down of Victoria wharf which led to the demise of Victoria's economic might, given that it was through this wharf that West Cameroonians imported and exported without having to pay taxes to a different province, region, or nation; the programmed collapse of Cameroon Bank, which made available inexpensive loans without the reigning bribery and corruption in existing banks; the unfortunate but deliberate transformation of our police force into an disorderly bunch even as the unique West Cameroon Police Mobile Wing Force was being disbanded; the arrival of gendarmes and "uniform brutality," divide and rule, and the nation's only state of emergency so far, an expression which belies what we experienced during those months.

I was doing just that—thinking, questioning and looking back—as I marveled at the beautiful weather while looking up at the peak of Mount Fako which was still buried under a heavily dense cloud, signs that the rain was far from over. Yet it had just rained and the air smelled fresh, with a cooling effect in the nostrils. This was my favorite season, unlike the dry season with all that dryness, heat, and humidity in the air, depending on the city in which one finds oneself at the time. The dryness is what I dread for it makes it difficult for one to breathe; it is as if the air scrapes the inside of one's nostrils as it streams through. I was sitting on the balcony of the top guest room of my elderly friend's two-storey building around Mile 17 Buea Road, enjoying the view all around me with my brain racing. It was too much for me to swallow with indifference: the name of my little country which today, on the map, looks like a poorly drawn triangle with a hump on the back, had been changed one time too many for me to continue ignoring this practice. It seemed like an exercise in futility to me as it led to nothing significant in particular other than more expenses on the part of an already financially challenged government. Now, for example, they had to immediately do away with countless letterheads with the country's old name on them and pay expensively to print new ones. In keeping with this ridiculous culture of waste, they would award the contract to a fraudulent contractor, from overseas, embarrassingly, with relations to someone in a position of power. They would also have to carve new rubber stamps used as government seals and so much more, but what are these in terms of cost and waste compared to the impending redesigning of the country's currency so that it carries the portrait of the new leader? The waste becomes obvious when one realizes that they do this just to satisfy the ego of a new president who has hardly achieved anything for the nation yet, unlike his mentor and predecessor whose portrait on our currency apparently scared him.

I was just a kid the previous times this happened, yet I had to struggle to get used to the new name of my beloved country, only to begin all over again as a young adult this time, as my country's name is changed, once more, on the whim of the president, it seemed to me. As a result, the nation had migrated nominally from Southern Cameroons through West Cameroon in the Federation of Cameroon, then The United Republic of Cameroon, and ultimately to The Republic of Cameroon; quite a journey, and were these nominal landmarks geographical settings, that would have amounted to quite a destination covered. Even then, that was the last straw: the ultimate nominal destination seemed to ignore the fact that there were two Cameroons in the beginning and that got me concerned. Yes, there were two Cameroons at the start—Southern Cameroons and La République du Cameroun—and through all the other names this duality of the nation's character, though one country, was always acknowledged. However, this last change gave the country the name one of the members was bearing before our reunification. "Something must be wrong here," I mused to myself. I was determined, whenever I could make time, to talk to my father about all this, which seemed to be a plan just falling in place. He should know better given his age; they were the ones who were there when Cameroon was born. I was around, yes, but still too young to understand what was going on. Like virtually every child, all I was interested in was the next thing with which to placate my molars. What was all this about anyway? Why do they have to keep changing the name of our country for no obvious reason? I hated it because of the way it left me feeling empty and ungrounded. It would be interesting hearing how my father would explain this.

Listening to our parents and grandparents talk was a lot of fun, and they always did talk. It was their way of educating us while directing our growth, their way of handing down to posterity the people that we were and are supposed to be, our identity so to say. They shared many different tales with us: about tortoise and hare racing, for example, with the slow tortoise finally emerging the winner because of its trickery. There was the tale about chameleon and dog being messengers from the supreme deity with a message for humankind about life and death. The issue was whether humans should die at all or live forever. The slow chameleon emerged winner because dog ran into free food, began gorging itself, and forgot about its business. It wasted time eating until chameleon got to man first and drummed the message of death. Ever since then, humans have to live to a certain age and then die. We also heard of world wars, yet as a child I never could figure out what they meant by that. Something would have to have gone very wrong with everyone on earth for everyone to be fighting against everyone else in a full-blown war. Yet there was proof in most homes that the war did not take place around where we lived; in fact, our grandparents, we found out, were instead carried away by the white man, for them to fight in other places far away from home. Of all places where our grandparents fought and died for no reason that mattered to us, as Africans, the name "Boma" stood out. I had heard of this place so many times that I could just not forget the name. However, it was a long time after, much later on in life, during one of my history classes, that I came to realize the "Boma" our grandparents talked about so often after the war, was in fact "Burma." This notwithstanding, all we ever learnt from our parents and grandparents was that it was a big war in which white people were killing white people and even the blacks were killing the whites. "So many people died," was always the final note about this mysterious war, the beginnings of which nobody seemed to know anything about, or else they never shared it.

Another passing fad of the war was the familiarization of the saying about old and durable things with the modifier "German," preceding them." It then dawned on the younger generation that to describe something as "German" was tantamount to guaranteeing its durability: "that German pair of shoes," or "that German motor-cycle." The times were reasonably good and stable, at least so it seemed to me as a child, but for these name changes at the government level that seemed to haunt me as if it was a duty of mine to find out why this was happening every so often comparatively speaking.

Far back in time, way back even before this name change became an issue with me, when I became aware of myself as a living entity, I was only a child of about four growing up in the coastal town of Buea at the foot of Mount Fako, a dormant volcano, 4070 metres high, which erupts from time to time. Buea was then the administrative headquarters of Southern Cameroons, which, in fact, the British administered from Lagos, Nigeria, at the time, since they considered it economical to do that instead of managing the affairs of

Southern Cameroons from another town or city out of neighbouring Nigeria. The name and territory known as Southern Cameroons emerged after what was recognized as Kamerun, under the Germans, was partitioned into two, the bigger half given to France and the smaller and less populated to the British. This was after WWI, during which the allied forces defeated Germany. These successful forces went ahead, seized all German territories overseas, and handed them as compensation to the allied nations who had been victorious in the war. The brains behind this do not like using the word "compensation" because of what it reveals about their activities in these territories, so they prefer calling them United Nations trust territories while claiming they were only being managed by these allied countries, like Britain and France, until they could be administratively independent. Who sets the standard of being administratively independent or capable remains a mystery known only to those western countries involved in the war and its ensuing resolutions. The peoples they were to administer did not seem to matter, and so like cattle they bandied them here and there according to the whims of foreign power brokers. Accordingly, the smaller part of Kamerun under Britain came to be known as Southern Cameroons and the part under France as La République du Cameroun.

I could remember myself as a child growing up in the town of Buea. My father, Philip, being a young police officer with an equally young family, occupied a two-room apartment in one section of the Police Barracks referred to as Old Barracks. The apartment was part of Line 1 as addresses were given at the time in the barracks. The buildings were arranged in long rows behind each of which stood the kitchen, followed by the next line of houses in another row. On the extreme left, on the edge of the barracks and between every two rows of houses stood the toilets and the lone pump from which the residents did their laundry and fetched drinking water. In front of my father's apartment (I think I should rather use the word "unit" as "apartment" conveys an overpowering sense of luxury or comfort which even the best of these units did not offer), which was in Line 1, there in the distance, stood the stone bungalow of the Inspector of Police. A small motorway and an equally small but neatly kept lawn separated the bungalow from the barracks. A neatly trimmed hedge also surrounded the bungalow and its lawn. The inspector at the time was a certain Inspector Anie. The difference in rank with the rest of the policemen and women was obvious. It came across from the style and structure of the inspector' bungalow, and from the way his yard was neatly kept. The design of his uniform was another pointer. It was obvious he was in charge of the rest of the barracks. There was order.

Life in the barracks was interesting to me as a child growing up. All I had to do was eat, and then, as an observer, be a part of the different official activities that involved all the police officers and sometimes even their families: how I loved walking by my father when, for example, he went to pick up his supplies from the supplies' room! It must have been once or twice a year that the police officers went to their supplies' room to be issued supplies. In the Police Barracks in Buea, the supplies room was a one room building which had the interior floor sloping in downward at about a 75-degree angle. Inside, it looked more like an unfinished grave belonging to one of those supposedly rich men whose children display their wealth on the occasion of their death by having the interior of their graves cemented as if that prevents decay or something. A man was usually standing down below this roofed pit-of-a-room and then the officers, on a first come first serve basis, would walk in one at a time and call out their shoe size. The man in the hole would twist around a couple of times and finally pick up a pair of shoes with the laces tied together and hand it over to the waiting police officer along with several other items. This twisting around, picking up and handing over of items would go on and on with the queue growing shorter until it was my father's turn and I would inch in forward with him to the edge of the grave. The hole looked very deep to me at the time, and so I was always afraid of the chances of me losing my footing and falling in over the cliff of boots.

"Size twelve!" my father would call out.

"Here we go!" the man in the hole always answered back after a few seconds of twisting and turning around.

There were two pairs: an ordinary plain black pair of formal wear for parades and a pair of boots, with hubs on the soles like nail crowns, for emergencies. Then there were other accessories: a shoe brush with thick soft bristles, cans of polish, a yellow piece of soft cloth for shinning the shoe with, along with a liquid substance in a can with the brand name, Brasso. They used Brasso for polishing the heavy bronze buttons on the uniforms at the time, belt buckles and the likes to sheen. As my father and I walked back home with our supplies, chatting over things that did not always make sense to me then, I remember on several occasions wondering about who it was who was so kind and generous to be distributing free shoes and stuff to my father and his colleagues.

Another barrack activity I used to enjoy was called "Fatigue." Fatigue was always on Saturday mornings. The sound of the whistle, one of those Southern Cameroons Police officers always carried in their left breast pocket and connected by a chain to one of their topmost shirt buttons, would be heard a couple of times, and all the police constables in the barracks would emerge from their homes dressed for manual work, each brandishing a machete. In different groups of about three or four pooled together by chance, as they emerged from their houses, they would walk to different sites in the barracks where they would assemble and exchange greetings and pleasantries for a while before they would begin weeding. It was usually along the streets leading in and out of the barracks. They would work for a while before breaking up and returning to their homes. I always wondered why they called it "fatigue" since the word always left the image of a tired person on my mind instead of a cleaning exercise for our surroundings.

The focus of all barrack activities to me was the parade rehearsals, when, as always, the men, and not more than several women who had just joined the police force, would line up on the barrack's lone football field and practice marching. I enjoyed the slow march more. The officers kind of leaned slightly backwards and would kick out a leg at a time, in short swift strides as if responding by reflex to a blow on the patella. The rehearsal started about two weeks to the national feast day. About a week to the event, the police band from the West Cameroon Police College in Mutengene would also show up for the rehearsals. I loved admiring the men and women of the band in their perfectly white uniforms. We, boys of my age and I, had heard that Commissioner Joseph Walters of then West Cameroon Police was in charge of the Police College in Mutengene, from where the Police band came. Since I did not know where Mutengene was or what it looked like, I painted a picture of Mutengene on my mind, dominated by a huge campus, the West Cameroon Police College. As children, we admired Commissioner Walters for his ways: disciplined, stern, and tough as a true superintendent should be. As a Cameroonian, he stood out because of how fair skinned he was; he could easily pass for one of those white men we used to see in their uniforms sitting behind chauffeured police cars. To my friends and I, this man epitomized success in every way; this was because of the manner in which he carried himself while sitting behind his chauffeured police car. We could tell he had a lot of power: one of the few, if not the only other police commissioner besides Commissioner Ntune. Commissioner Ntune was so powerful he was the only police officer whose residence was in the Government Residential Area where only powerful men in the government resided; the G.R.A. they called it for short. It took a long time after Ntune and Walters for other police commissioners to begin emerging. There was Noster, Vando, Chiabi and Kumfa, to name a few. My generation will always remember Commissioner Kumfa for the trauma he caused us as young men in the seventies as he went around arresting young men and women from nightclubs and having them detained if they were without identification papers or suspected of prostituting. By this time, however, it was no longer the West Cameroon Police force; it had now been adulterated with crude La République tactics like this arbitrary arrest of citizens in the name of keeping the peace. Why were we obliged to carry identification papers on our person at all times as if we were in a state of emergency? Why was it not acceptable for someone who did not have his on him to explain that he had forgotten his documents at home and yet be able to answer correctly to other security questions that established he was a respectable peace-loving citizen? This approach to life was far ahead of its time, even for today's dastardly hour when murderous men go around killing innocent people because of differences in the beliefs they hold. There is still something wrong about just surprising people and dumping decent citizens behind a dirty military truck simply because their identity cards are not on them. In civilized societies, officers of the forces of law and order give such culprits a number of hours to present the document at any police station, having taken their car number or something of value from them. This was and still is not the case with our forces of law and order whose members enjoy harassing their citizens instead of just doing their job. Usually half-educated and rustic in their approach, this is their moment to show the victims that they too are of some importance and so they make citizens to beg and even bribe to regain their freedom.

Beyond the parades, another attraction for us as residents of the Police Barracks was the dog parade and displays. Huge German shepherd dogs from the Police College in Mutengene were usually brought to the police barracks soccer field for display so the public was made aware of what these dogs could do. They obeyed difficult and sometimes coded commands from their handlers and would jump through, over, and even force their way underneath obstacles that left the crowd cheering in disbelief how animals could be so intelligent. The main attraction, however, was when the dogs displayed the use of their powerful sense of smell to track and apprehend a criminal from among several other people. The handlers would make a dog to pick up a particular smell from a crime scene and then they would turn it loose. The dog would wind its way through a maze of obstacles, changing its course from time to time until it arrived at a scene with a number of idlers and it would isolate and grab the criminal by his sleeve. The crowd would go wild with excitement. It was also interesting to learn that these dogs, like our parents, had ranks; see the huge buckets of rice, stew, and meat that they gobbled up during their meal hour.

In those days, looking back now and comparatively speaking, the rank of a police officer had power attached to it. As a police corporal, for example, one had about two or three other police officers answerable to one, and as a sergeant, about forty-fifty. In this light, an inspector of police in those days was a very high-ranking officer with so many police officers from the rank of sergeant down to lance corporals under his command. These men and the few women among their ranks were nice and friendly to members of the public. In fact, one was brought up to understand that police officers were not only servants of the state but also friends of the public, and they were. Because of this servant of the state/citizen relationship between the police and members of the public, the police officer's job was a lot easier to perform. They relied on assistance, especially in the form of information from the public, for solving crimes and keeping the peace, unlike today when the police officer is an enemy outright. This brings to my mind an incident I once witnessed in recent years in Old Town Bamenda in front of where Day Spring, a bar, used to be. There was a *suya* spot I used to frequent in the 90's whenever some repairs were being done on my car radio—extracting a stuck cassette, replacing a blown fuse or something of that sort. Once as I sat there munching and chatting with others when a police bus swung in from the Commercial Avenue end of the street and skidded to a halt right in front of us but across the street. Police officers, about five of them in number, jumped out brandishing revolvers and swinging into action in the manner of some modern day anti-terrorist group. A few shots rang in the air from police guns to indicate they were serious. Several police officers ran into a building across from us, and after about five minutes emerged with a half-naked young man. They dragged him into their bus and zoomed off, obviously feeling victorious even as the small crowd that had gathered looked on with animosity. I could not help wondering if all that bravado was just to arrest a teenager who sold marijuana and had never touched a gun in his life unlike other distributors in some countries who carry semi-automatic weapons. This was a most shocking display of police inefficiency in my opinion, as there was no tact involved other than a display of brute force. Had the young man been armed and willing to fight back then a number of innocent civilians enjoying themselves would have been in the line of fire and might have ended up hurt or otherwise. A well-coordinated raid would have been at a time when there was the least number of civilians around and so on, but that is our police force today; it is all about showing off and intimidating people and nothing about tact, nothing about upholding the law. Otherwise how does one explain the fact that even senior police officers go around, even in churches on Sunday, brandishing police radios that in more sophisticated societies are hardly seen unless in cases of emergencies? How would the public know they are powerful officers if they do not parade their more likely than otherwise démodé equipment in this manner?

The Southern and later West Cameroon Police Force, on the other hand, was exemplary in every way, for which reason I started nursing hopes of becoming a police officer myself someday. I was always very happy in the company of young police officers who were my father's peers. There was, for example, Mr. Jacob Anye, Mr. Asukwo, Mr. Martin Massa, Mr. John Biaka, Mr. Ade who was a long distance runner, Mr. Nfor who was much into fashion at the time, and later on an elderly police man who was resident in Buea town also, Pa Motombi. I used to admire Mr. Nfor's private leather shoes, which were pointed at the tip in a near ridiculous manner it seemed to me, but it was the trend then. They were thorough gentlemen and cared about each other. Outstanding was the respect they had for their uniforms: a police officer could never be seen in a public drinking spot in uniform—never! There was the police canteen at the Long Street Soppo end of the barracks' field, which was itself on the South-West end of the barracks. Here officers in uniform could pause for a drink or a game of table tennis. Members of their families could also use these facilities, and police kids assembled here for their annual Christmas parties during which they participated in a variety of games that yielded spectacular prizes. I always remember winning a beautiful dinner set once. These opportunities and facilities were also available for the warders in their own barracks across from the Police Barracks. Both barracks were separated mainly by the lone-tarred road, which, then, divided Buea into two almost equal halves. The road, meandered its way up from Mile 17 only to form the top stroke of the uppercase letter "T" at the Station—the right half continuing on to Buea Town, and the other half snaking on to Bokwaongo and beyond, past the sole radio station West Cameroon had at the time—Radio Buea.

Radio Buea brings to mind names like Mark Neboh, Aaron Ngoe, and Tatah Mentan with fantastic programs like "Request Time" which, if I can recall well, came up on Saturdays, and "Meet the Patients" on Sunday mornings. These are examples of landmark journalists, reporters, producers, and programs that made our weekends enjoyable, especially as there were no television stations at the time. Mark Neboh was the indefatigable Chief of programs and news, Aaron Ngoe was the personification of the very entertaining program "Meet the Patients," while Tatah Mentan was in charge of the program "Variety Show," which was a medley of pop music, politics, and events. With such a broad base, Tatah Mentan, the honest, unequivocal, and more often than not fearlessly vituperative social critic, could nibble at or bite into events and personages of the hour depending on the nature and gravity of their trespasses. He would do that, only to turn around and dampen his causticity with the latest pop music, but he had said what he wanted to say. How he escaped Ahidjo's gestapo remains a mystery. With such entertaining and equally didactic programs from Radio Buea, the only radio station in the whole of West Cameroon at the time, families used to sit together and with such addictive fervor follow these programs and relishing every bit.

Sundays were my favorite days of the week. My mother would return from Muea market just on time for "Meet the Patients." We would gather around her on a mat on our verandah eating sugarcane and munching away at mangoes and other delicacies she had returned with from the market as we laughed at the different remarks made by the patients whom Aaron Ngoe was skillfully interviewing. The journalists and producers usually went to the Buea Hospital week after week from ward to ward recording this program. Aaron Ngoe, it has to be Aaron Ngoe, both names and in this order, else one is talking about somebody else, would visit the accident ward this week, the maternity ward next week, the children's ward subsequently, and so on. He would talk to the patients about their health before giving them the opportunity to communicate their thoughts, greetings, and other messages to friends and loved ones back at home. Then it was finally time for Aaron Ngoe to have the patients request a particular record for him to play for their entertainment; it took a great soul to come up with this program.

We loved listening to some of the patients gasping for air as they addressed themselves to family members and friends, then we went on to enjoy their choice of music played for their "listening and dancing pleasure." I usually enjoyed a woman seizing the opportunity to inform her extended relatives that she had just put to bed and she and the baby were doing fine. Questions asked around the child's name, why the choice of record, or where the child's father was, brought forth some interesting answers from the women in the maternity ward. Our pleasure peaked when our father happened to be around and joined the rest of the family in enjoying the weekend in this manner. He himself used to crack some jokes related to the different answers given by the patients that would send us roaring with laughter. Life was good: our parents were always there for us. They went to work by 8:00am and returned by 3:30pm with only a thirty-minute break in between from 12:00 noon to 12:30pm. Accordingly, they were able to spend the rest of the day with their families gardening, helping the kids with homework, or just simply playing around with the children. In fact, this is how my father got me hooked on soccer such that it almost became a profession for me.

The parades and dog displays done with, there were moments I considered special when I used to join the players of the Police football team for training. By this time, Southern Cameroons had migrated from being administered in tandem with Nigeria and was now independent but as part of the new nation called the Federal Republic of Cameroon which contained the French speaking part or East Cameroon, and the English speaking part or West Cameroon. Having thus migrated nominally, the police team, accordingly, was referred to as the West Cameroon Police Football team and precisely Police United. I was their pacer from time to time. At barely four or five years of age, I used to run round the soccer field, my father handing me peppermint tablets from time to time, as I was on course. I jogged round and round that field tirelessly, with the players gasping behind me, until my father would ask me to stop.

I used to marvel at the football itself—a coat of leather surrounding a reddish bladder full of air. The leather jacket was then laced tight at one end in the manner of an American football but for the fact that this soccer ball was round in shape. From time to time, the bladder inside the leather jacket exploded from too much pressure when two players smashed into the ball at the same time. I used to love picking up the ball and smelling the leather with Goalkeeper Njomo of Police United standing and laughing at my childish fancy and me; he, like all these men, was nice. I continue to wonder if it was their training as police officers that made them so nice and gentle or if fate just pooled together some wonderful men for the young police force. Mr. Njomo must have been trying to make a goalkeeper out of me, but I would rather stand there smelling the ball instead of tossing or kicking it back to him—a retriever who took the ball to his own destination instead of returning it to his trainer. With our migration from Nigeria, for the first time I saw, even with the eyes of a child, the death of an already established maintenance culture that was in place. The police team had a vehicle that was fascinating to my eyes as a child because it came across as a house on wheels. This vehicle, unlike anything I had ever seen before, had compartments for different players. I remember feeling very sad once when I walked past the police garage, which used to be close to Long Street Soppo and the road to the hospital, and saw this van standing there obviously now abandoned. I learned it was bad when I asked what the matter was.

"But it had been bad before and was repaired," I queried the police officer in charge of the maintenance garage.

"That's true son, but this time we have been told there are no parts and the money is not there to have it fixed." It was painful to see a van that once symbolized the police team stand there day and night until the wrath of the elements changed its colour even before rust settled in to finalize its process of decay.

2

Life as police children growing up in the barracks was fun. It was a huge police family as we followed through with the different activities. I was also growing up, and soon it was time for school and my doting father had me registered at the Roman Catholic Mission (RCM) School Buea Town where my older sister, Rita, and my young uncle, Vince, were already pupils. My mother's life became a nightmare as she fussed about my safety. Her worry was about how I would go across the main highway that formed part of Bongo's Square safely since the school was on the other side of town. My mother would worry until I would show up running with my writing board flapping behind me on a string as I returned home from school with chalk marks all over my uniform. I always soiled myself as I struggled to preserve my day's work from school for my parents to see. "Look up, look down, quickly look up again and then run across if there is no vehicle approaching. If you see a car coming, wait for it to go past, then begin all over again," both my parents briefed me on a daily basis as I was about leaving for school. My father recited this refrain just before he left for work in the morning, even if, as usual, it was not time for me to leave. My mother who walked me almost a third of the distance repeated the safety mantra just before she let me off, about a hundred metres to the dangerous highway. She could have as well just walked me across the road before returning, but some little thing in her made her leave me virtually next to the road. May be she was trying to teach me to assume a certain degree of responsibility—may be!

My mother's anxiety about my safety soared beyond limits when a car killed Kebila, the son of another police officer living in the barracks, as he tried going across the highway at a spot then referred to as Petrol Point. This was the location of a lone petrol filling station at a point of the highway today referred to as Bongo's Square, named after then President Bongo of Gabon was received on a presidential visit at that spot in Buea sometime in the '60s. Kebila, we heard, had gone to purchase meat for the family from the cold store just across the highway when on his way back a vehicle ran him over. We heard of how he died on the spot, the meat he had bought strewn all over the tarmac. I never forgot Kebila, nor did I forget his tall father who was so fair in complexion such that we, police children in the barracks, compared his eyes to those of a cat because of the color, which deviated from the traditional black with a certain shimmering if not glassy quality.

I will never know the last straw. May be it was because my father's small family was expanding and needed more room, or maybe it was Kebila's tragic death and my parents just could not go on taking any risks; all I remember is that shortly after the tragedy of Kebila's death, we moved to Buea Town. The move stands out in my mind for some strange reason. Moreover, it was the first time I felt the pangs of parting from people I had come to develop an affinity for, not to say love. The number was increasing, and so beyond Mr. John Biaka, and Mr. Ade for example, there was now Mr. Gregory Njawe who played on the Police United Football squad and always gave me a twenty-five francs coin whenever he met me, and then there was another police man with whom my father had a nickname—Bojado. I also remember a young policewoman who lived in New Barracks. New and Old Barracks were just side-by-side, and their names tell which was built first. Comfort was this woman's name, but we always referred to her as Ma Comfort as a sign of respect which our culture demands. As much as my parents permitted me to visit the close family friends we had, of all the bachelors and unmarried women, I loved visiting Ma Comfort most. Her single room smelled beautifully, and I enjoyed the scent of what I discovered later on to be nail polish, which seemed always to be in the air. She was dark-skinned, beautiful, and gentle. Then there were the children in the barracks whom I was going to miss, especially Tita, a boy of my age, who lived in Line 2 with his father, Mr. Vando, and then there were the Anomas: Ernest, Eric, Elizabeth, and Valentine. For some reason, I had become attached to the children of this family who were living about four lines further down in New Barracks; I was not sure I would ever see them again. But for Valentine who was younger, the rest were in varying degrees older than I was, but strangely, I mattered to them albeit the age difference, for which reason I became very fond of them also.

Another thing I was going to miss were the emergencies that erupted from time to time. It had dawned on me that the whistling had coded messages. Some times when the whistle went, our fathers would hurry out to the motorable road separating New and Old into two different barracks. At other times, they took their time and sauntered out minutes after the sound of the whistle had faded in the distance, yet at other times, they rushed. The rushing culminated in near pandemonium with mothers and wives rushing and preparing little snacks—fried groundnuts, boiled eggs, biscuits, bread, milk in tins and so on—which would be arranged in the men's knapsacks. My mother always did this for my father. Meanwhile, my father would fold and roll his thick raincoat that easily doubled for a blanket into a thick yet manageable column. He would then get into his thick woolen grey uniform shirt and heavily starched police khaki trousers, the leggings of which he would burry into his boots and then use khaki coloured puttees to hold them in place. Then he would now tie together the loose edges of his raincoat, forming a thick kind of bandanna, which he threw over his head across his shoulder like the strap of a bag after he had strapped on his knapsack. Then his water bottle would also go over his head in the opposite direction, his bayonet would go to a sheath dangling behind from his right hip and then his helmet on his head. My father would then take from me his gun, which I had taken out of its traditional post behind the door leading into his bedroom. He would hug us all, and then nibble lightly at the tips of our thumbs asking us to stay well until his return. With everything said and done, he would step out and the darkness outside would quickly swallow him up from our view. When this happened by day, it left a kind of eerie feeling hanging over the barracks as young wives stepped off their verandas, in some cases with their children, to catch a last glimpse of their husbands who soon lost their individualities as they merged into the flowing stream of identically dressed uniformed officers. When it happened at night, as was the case this time, the men disappeared into the darkness quicker and only the heavy sound of their hobnailed boots crunching into the gravel and the tarmac would hang in the air. They were all usually ominously quiet at this time, given that they knew they were heading into danger. Then one after the other seven-ton trucks loaded with heavily armed police officers would rumble out of the barracks. The wives were more often than not at a loss as to their husbands' whereabouts, sometimes for months even. All everyone knew was that the officers were out because of *maquisards* (terrorists) who had attacked a village or something. Tombel was a dreaded name at the time because of all the killings we heard took place there, and so mention of it conjured frightful thoughts in my head; stories held it to be a notorious *maquisard* bastion.

Once my father left like this, and it must have been months after and he was yet to be back, nor was there any news about him for my mother. My mother, then a young wife, bundled my younger sister and me and took off to Lobe to my father's older brother, Pa Peter Awah who was working with Pamol at the time, a kernel oil producing company that employed thousands of workers from all over the country. My mother wanted him to know his brother had gone missing according to her since she had not heard from him for months nor did the police inspector have any words about him.

At Lobe, my younger sister fell sick and my mother had to take her to the hospital. We had been trekking towards the hospital for a while when I heard the roaring sound of a vehicle's engine coming from behind. I turned and saw a vehicle indeed; it was speeding towards us, the dust it provoked gave me to understand, but it was far in the distance. My head turned a couple of times more as I unconsciously estimated its speed and distance with each turn of my head so as to determine when it would be close enough for me to see the passengers. When at last I turned one more time, the vehicle was a police Land Rover with its windshield folded onto its bonnet to make room for a mounted machine gun; it was speeding past us. I yelled as I recognized my father behind the gun. The vehicle stopped in the distance. My father jumped off and ran to us. They were in a hurry and he would be home soon was all I could remember him saying as he bade us goodbye and ran back to the Land Rover which took off leaving behind a thick trail of dust. My mother, who was already weeping, walked on slowly after the dust settled.

Some time passed before we returned to Buea; may be just a few days, my child's mind perceived certain things differently, especially the concepts of time and distance. I say this because years after I visited the police barracks and distances I thought, as a child, were so far, I found out were not that far after all. The walk from our house in the barracks to the police canteen is an example. I got a better perspective of these things as I grew older. It was not long after we returned from Lobe before a group of police men returned to the barracks from the long and suspense-laden expedition into the heart of *Maquisard* land—Tombel—as we were given to understand. By the way, I loved visiting my uncle in Lobe. He was in charge of the canteen, and he would let me eat sweets until my mouth was sore. This was an incredible treat to me since I usually had sweets only on occasions as for some strange reason my father always wanted to control my sugar in-take, although he enjoyed making me eat raw slices of onion strands. I did not particularly like the experience as its poignant taste and flavor culminated in a strange simmering or effervescent effect up inside the bridge of my nose, causing me to sneeze repeatedly with tears welling in my eyes. My father would laugh gently as if satisfied I had learnt an intended lesson.

My father and his older brother really loved each other and so we were always in constant touch. In fact, they looked for the slightest excuse to visit each other, and so when on annual furlough, my father would visit his brother in Lobe and spend some time with him. I used to be amused by the way my uncle treated my father. Upon returning from a trip to Lobe, my father would bring out gift after gift sent virtually to every single member of the family. As a child, I used to be puzzled when my father would show us his own shirts bought for him by his brother. I usually ended up smiling and being even more perplexed because I knew that adults bought things for children because the latter did not have jobs, yet here was my father's older brother buying shirts for him. It made me see my father like some kind of child too when his brother was concerned. This exchange of gifts between families was wonderful; it reminded us of the true meaning of a family even though we were so far away from each other.

Another opportunity for a visit to Pa Lobe, as my uncle Pa Peter came to be known, or Pa Buea as my father was in turn referred to, came with the arrival of a new child in either family. Mammy Lobe would visit Buea with the latest addition to the Lobe family when the child was a few months old and capable of withstanding the trip and she would spend months with her "younger husband" and vice versa, when it was my mother's turn. Each wife returned home refreshed and spoiled with money and gifts, then the men would take their turn and come and go when on leave from work, which was just about once a year. The cycle continued for years and years even after the government transferred Pa Buea to Bamenda. It was the practice at the time that as a civil servant grew older and closer to retirement, the government sent him or her back or closer to his or her native soil so he or she could effectively prepare for this phase of life.

It was a police department seven ton truck with tarpaulin that came to move our things when the hour for my father to leave the police barracks came. My father, with the help of a few friends, neatly packed his scanty furniture and other belongings into the truck. My parents sat in front carrying the kids with them—Rita, Emmanuel, Anthonia and baby Judith. Vince, my young uncle was alone in the back of the truck enjoying the freedom of being away from my parents' control, even for only a few minutes.

I remember how this uncle of mine came to live with us. He suddenly showed up one day at dusk, accompanied by two women in loincloths. My parents were glad to have him. He came with a small portmanteau as they called them then: a box made of cardboard, which was almost as small as those small metal boxes local metal men used to produce for kids to use in transporting their books to and from school. He also had a raffia bag hanging from his shoulders. Out of this bag, he took out two little packets of biscuits, which he gave me. Each packet contained four pairs of biscuits between each of which pair was a yellowish substance like some sort of sugary margarine-like combination. It tasted good, but it is no longer in the market after all these years. It was now a new era in Vince's life with him being a part of his sister's, brother-in-law's, and their children's lives.

Bonaberi Quarter, Buea Town, the name of our new neighbourhood, was a completely new setting. Unlike in the

Police Barracks, the houses were not regimented nor were our lives going to be. The streets were stony and the indigenes built their houses on either side facing the stony streets. In most cases, the top half of the walls were of wood, whereas, about four to five feet off the floor was built of zinc sheets that came from casks that once carried tar it seemed to me. I never found out why, but I guessed the tar-coated zinc withstood the heavy and long lasting rainy onslaughts in Buea better than any treated wood would which would soon become wet and then decay would set in. This always happened with most "calaboat" houses, as these wooden structures were known. Not processed in any way against water, but for the occasional painting, before long the wooden walls started decaying with sections crumbling from time to time as if termites were to blame, but Buea did not seem to have any termite problems. In the end, once beautiful walls would develop holes and attendant patches here and there as the landlords struggled to keep their houses in the leasing market. In the extreme, there were houses tilting at dangerous angles with some propped in position by poles, yet people lived in them. Buea, however, is not a typical windy town, the characteristic long lasting drizzles of the rainy season notwithstanding.

A Bamileke man owned our new home and painted it all black. As if to give his house a name, he wrote on the edge of the roof "BELANTENZIE." I never found out the meaning. The building had about five other tenants. Interestingly, they were all police families. There was Mr. Martin Massa, our direct neighbor, who with my father occupied the two sections facing the Catholic Mission direction of town, and then there was Mr. Jacob Anye, Mr. Asukwo, Mr. Bambod, and a fat Bamileke police officer Mr. Jean on the side facing the mountain. Mr. Jean, the fat policeman, had a beautiful young wife who was always at home sewing and knitting. Our family quickly got settled down with my father going off to work as usual—the distance being about the same as when we were at the barracks—and we the children to school. There was no motor road to endanger our daily trips to and from school, so our parents now had some peace of mind and were determined to focus on raising us; again, school was really close to home this time.

Meanwhile, in the political arena, the name Ahidjo was becoming a household name instead of Foncha, as was the case before, when Foncha was living in that huge German-built building located just below Upper Farms called The Prime Minister's Lodge and rumoured to have about seventy rooms. I say rumoured because we heard of the number of rooms but not of the authority who did the counting, even though we went to school with Foncha's children. John Ngu Foncha was then prime minister of West Cameroon, and his name, like Ahidjo's was no longer a personal name but an official title. So it was normal for us to answer to the question "What do you want to become when you grow up?" with "Ahidjo," simply. It was later on in life that we found out "Ahidjo" was the president's personal name. Yes, we were in school with some Foncha kids, but one never, for some odd reason, asked them if indeed the prime minister's lodge had seventy rooms. The building, perched majestically at the foot of Mount Fako, has a commanding view of much of Buea and beyond even. I remember visiting the lodge once as a child with my father when Foncha was its occupant. The Mobile Wing officer stationed at the gate surprised me—he was friendly. Although we knew the police to be our friends, the West Cameroon Police Mobile Wing officers were dreaded because of the extreme discipline their training instilled in them; besides, they were neat, trimmed, and looked rugged. Stories of incredible feats they could perform circulated. One of such stories made quite an impression on my childhood imagination. I had learned that as part of their training, these men were expected to jump out of a moving vehicle without hurting themselves; it was part of their training and they had to master this phase especially. I imagined a vehicle which, while just a passenger, made me dizzy as things sped by, then to imagine a Mobile Wing officer jumping out of a moving vehicle and not getting hurt caused me to hold them in such awe. I was not surprised then, when I heard it was an elite paramilitary group that only the best of the best police officers could dream of ever belonging to, given the intensive training involved.

Yes, the Mobile Wing officer at the entrance into the premises of the prime minister's lodge saluted, relaxed and was at ease when he saw my father. I later on found out he was able to relax not only because my father was a policeman himself, but also because they had known each other way back in primary school. I marveled about his being a Mobile Wing officer.

Thus, we heard of John Ngu Foncha, of Muna, of Jua, and of Endeley, whose lengthy initials I used to enjoy as a child; yes, I enjoyed the smooth flow of the initials: "Dr. E. M. L. Endeley." It occurred to me that the latter had so many names all to himself. Meanwhile, with a lot of endearment, people always added "Short" in front of John Ngu Foncha's names until it became almost a title. He was small in stature but a determined and poised politician. In like manner, his names had to be given in full at all times for some strange reason. It may be because they were all short names or that is how they appeared in our civics books then and so we studied them like that. The political scenario was comparatively speaking so stable the names of ministers could be printed in textbooks; they were sure to be there for years before being changed if ever. Saoudou Daoudu, for example, was Minister of Armed Forces for eighteen years or thereabouts; Christian Bongwa, Minister of Transport, and Simon Achidi Achu Minister of Justice; Felix Tonye Mbog, Minister of Youth and Sports, and so on. In any case, whatever was the reason, Foncha's names were always presented as "John Ngu Foncha." It was also because of his smallish build, which contrasted greatly with his successful political achievements, that the saying "small no be sick" became a household pep expression: a person's build has nothing to do with his potentials. After John Ngu Foncha, there were talks of Jua becoming prime minister—he did. Then there was a time it was Muna, although people talked of how he had betrayed Jua to Ahidjo in the process of getting the seat, and so the much respected and admired Jua had to move out of the prime minister's lodge for Muna to move in. Jua, compared to Muna, was short and fair in complexion whereas the other was dark skinned and tall, but Jua, it trickled down through the grapevine, was fearlessly brave. In fact, it was said that besides Professor Bernard Fonlon who was considered eccentric by some, and Albert Womah Mukong who was willing to die for the Southern Cameroons cause, he was the only one who could dare stand and tell the dreaded dictator, Ahidjo, in his face, what he thought of him or any of his policies. It is not surprising then that people suspected Ahidjo of having a hand in his death when it occurred suddenly and without any premonitions whatsoever.

3

All seemed to be well after a long while, then we learned Ahidjo had become the president of Cameroon and so the name of our country was to change into the Federal Republic of Cameroon, with the former Southern Cameroons known as West Cameroon. The story was that Southern Cameroons and Ahidjo's La République du Cameroun, which the British and the French used to administer, albeit separately, and so were English and French speaking respectively, had agreed to join and emerge as a nation. Before this merger, Ahidjo's Cameroun was known as La République du Cameroun, but its name was now to change to East Cameroon; West and East Cameroon were coming together to form a federation to be known as the Federal Republic of Cameroon/La République Fédéral du Cameroun. The word "reunion" flew around a lot, with faces smiling as they mentioned it, but there were others who were not so happy; they had wished we went the other way, which was join Nigeria in order to become a nation. It was again said the United Nations gave Southern Cameroons terrible choices as the people themselves had preferred a third choice which was denied them. Southern Cameroonians wanted to become independent on their own merit, but they were forced to choose between what the citizens believed to be two evils, and they went with what they considered the lesser evil they knew—the Republic of Cameroon. Southern Cameroon's experience with Nigeria had not been favourable; the Igbos were found to be too domineering we heard.

It was not long before Southern Cameroonians began experiencing the inferno into which reunion with La République was to transform. Because Southern Cameroons was already enjoying an incredibly high level of democracy and therefore order and freedom, citizens of La République du Cameroun (East Cameroon) started flooding into West Cameroon. We heard of the "dangerously notorious" political party UPC, as it was frighteningly known instead of its full name Union des Populations du Cameroun. There was talk of its members being on the run from the police, but nobody told us clearly why they were running away and people were reluctant believing what the government owned radio was saying. We heard of names which had immediately acquired mythical qualities as there were different stories bandied around about them: there was Um Nyobé, Gabriel Tabeu aka Wambo le Courant, Ntumazah, and the rest. We heard these "traitors" had taken to the bushes from where they were attacking innocent civilians going about their daily affairs, for which reason word trickled in on a daily basis about *maquisards* growing in numbers and being responsible for the unrest in East Cameroon. Again, nobody gave a convincing story as to why these people were on the run, as to why soldiers were burning down villages, with white soldiers participating, even as unarmed men and women were being slaughtered. People, following government propaganda, were always afraid of going to the fields to farm for fear of being seized and carried away by *maquisards*. We were given to think these were bad people who occupied the bushes hunting down and killing innocent villagers, as a result of which the police and the military had to go into the bushes from time to time to hunt them down in return. We heard they were mainly in East Cameroon, but were beginning to cross over into West Cameroon, which was stable and safer. Names of towns like Tombel, Loum, Mbanga, and Nkongsamba amongst others immediately struck a frightful note each time they were mentioned; they were *maquisards* strongholds according to the government. Accordingly, we heard of *maquisards* sporadically attacking places, even police stations and gendarme brigades in places like Loum, Tombel and Nkongsamba and killing the officers.

This atmosphere of fear notwithstanding, as children growing up in Buea, we loved to go out in search of different fruits regardless of the fact that the fruit trees belonged to different people. However, because these trees were usually away in the bushes on people's farm lots or seemingly abandoned pieces of land, even when we were sure they belonged to people, as opposed to being wild fruit trees, we did not care as part of the fun of the whole experience came from the owners chasing us away. We were certain we were faster than any farm owner could be, and so, although we felt tense as we executed these ventures, we were sure in the end we would be the winners running away with bag loads of mangoes especially. We also loved picking guavas on another piece of government land that used to be called West Farm. The new and current road to Bokwaongo behind the military camp in Long Street Soppo meanders through the heart of what used to be West Farm. In those days, it was a vast wilderness of bushes given value in our eyes only by the numerous guava trees with guava fruits of all sizes, colours, and flavors hanging from the branches. As children in the RCM (Roman Catholic Mission) Buea Station, otherwise known as "Slow School," we would sneak away from school at some odd hour to go pick guavas from West Farm. Usually we waited until when classes were on recess, or just at the end of the day when our teachers had asked us to go home. Instead of heading home, the group whose members had already identified themselves would converge on an agreed on spot to begin the trek into West Farm. We always made sure we had at least three members of the group who knew, purportedly, where exactly we were going. Much later on in life, I came to understand that even the very best guides amongst us did not know where exactly we were going; at best they had a vague picture of the direction and they only felt a sense of relief when we emerged somewhere within West Farm. West Farm extended from somewhere behind the RCM School Station, covering the land behind the General hospital all the way to the Juvenile detention unit in West Farm and up northwards all the way behind the Presidential Rest house in Buea and far in towards Bokwaongo. I never knew its confines away from the Catholic School premises; there was nothing with the intrinsic value to cause me to want to go that far, not the guavas for sure, and with the threat of the possibilities of *maquisards* snatching and making away with one, forget it. It was usually a traumatizing experience given that we were scared to death of potential encounters with "terrorists" in the bushes. We feared they could abduct us and that would be it. We moved from tree to tree tasting the fruits in search of trees with very sweet fruits. One would bite into the first fruit from a tree, savour a mouthful for a few seconds, spit it out in disgust if it were sour, and move on to the next tree. If it turned out to be sweet, one harvested the sizeable fruits and threw them into our bags. The fruits came in a variety of flavors and we named them according to our whims including the sour fruits that we treated with spite as if the fruits were to blame for conspiring with nature to turn out thus. The sweet fruit could be bright red inside, pale red, or whitish which some called coco or milk guava.

Talking about the juvenile detention unit in West Farm, come to think of it, West Cameroon had a fantastic penitentiary system. In Buea, for example, the penitentiary was divided into four separate units: Upper Farms, Middle Farms, Lower Farms, and West Farm. At Upper Farms, the prisoners were not dangerous; we came to understand somehow since the authorities permitted them to serve the public. In addition, they were people with short prison sentences who had a lot to benefit by being well behaved since it meant they went back home to their families on time without their sentences tampered with for different reasons such as fighting, attacking a prison officer, or attempting to break out. Accordingly, they had been imprisoned for minor offences. Their outfits as convicts were always very clean. They farmed vegetables like green beans, tomatoes, cabbages, and lettuce for example, and maintained cattle that made it possible for Upper Farms to produce pasteurized milk, which they bottled in pint sizes and sold to the public for twenty francs a bottle. They also produced butter. Upper Farms prison was located high up the lower rungs of Mount Fako; virtually everything about this unit sparkled clean under the control of Prison Superintendent Nju, with his beautiful Citroen car, which, as children, we called "an aeroplane car." This name was derived from the fact that when the engine of this particular model was turned off, the car sort of sank gently as if there were airbags that got deflated underneath, bringing the car's chassis to ground level, only for it to rise again to normal driving height when the engine was turned on. Cars were a rarity then and so one with such idiosyncratic qualities stood out.

Middle Farm, on the other hand, it would seem to me, was a maximum-security unit which housed dangerous criminals. They fell into two large groups: those on death row and those on hard labour. Prisoners from this unit rarely went out; those that qualified to go out as a work force were closely monitored. Prisoners in this unit were fenced in and had little contact with the outside world. Some of them, the majority, put on white shirts and shorts and white skullcaps. Their white uniforms had either blue or thin red stripes, which could only be identified at close range, running horizontally every two inches or so apart. As kids, we concluded that those with blue stripes were not as dangerous as those with red stripes were, and so one had to be careful in dealing with them. The most dangerous had on deep (almost navy) blue uniforms with "CC" written in white on their left breast area. The "CC" stood for "condemned criminal," and they were always chained at the ankles even within the prison yard. As an altar boy in the sixties, I came in contact with these people on Saturday mornings when the late Revered Father Anthony Van De Vlugt from St Anthony's Parish Buea Town would take me and sometimes Job Orji or may be Gervase Ndoko there as his altar boys for the celebration of Holy Mass. I simply could not, as a child, fathom how so many people could live fenced in in such a small space, but they did.

Lower Farms meanwhile, was also fenced in, but not like Middle Farm; whereas the former was casually fenced just to show where the Department of Prison's estate started and ended, the latter was fenced to hem in the prisoners for security reasons. Rows of barbed wire nailed onto wooden poles made up the fence at Lower Farm. The poles with about four rows of barbed wires running across were planted in the ground about ten metres apart to keep people out of the huge premises, somewhere in the middle of which yard stood several buildings crowded together like an island in a sea of farmed beds. Occasionally, a prisoner would be seen strolling about the place. I never found out what services Lower Farm Prisons rendered other than some scale of farming. I know they had some offices and a motor mechanic workshop and that was it. In a way, in the direction towards the mountain, it joined the warders' barracks, which formed a kind of horseshoe keeping Middle Farm Prison in check.

West Farm, we learned, was for juveniles, even though I never got close enough to see the juveniles detained there. One only saw some long buildings from the distance and that was it. It was always on my mind though as I wondered about what it was that a child would do and instead of his parents having him disciplined at home would have him sent to prison. This question bothered me until later when I understood what juvenile detention was all about. I never thought children could commit crimes against the state such that their parents would no longer matter and they would have to be tried and sentenced to a juvenile detention facility. The facility stood there far away in the distant bush with nothing appealing that could provoke one to visit it; the only family I once visited in West Farm was the Fielding family. Close by though, were the acres of bushes with guava trees all over the place that we would skip school to haunt. One never found out who owned the fruit trees, and why in such large numbers. At some other point in our history, given that it was on government property, one would have considered it some kind of government project turned sour as usual. Whatever the case, from "stealing" guavas to visiting friends with my father, it was always a huge relief to leave West Farm behind and head back into civilization without an encounter with the supposedly ubiquitous *maquisards*.

Once we, a group of schoolchildren, were guava hunting and saw a man in the distance who seemed to be walking towards us, so we scattered in every direction and ran away convinced our lives were on the line. Some of us emerged behind the Buea hospital, some behind our school, and yet others farther away. Not everyone knew well the paths in and out of West Farm. We never found out who the intruder was, even though we knew there was a short cut from Bokwaongo through West Farm into Long Street Small Soppo. Our fears seemed authenticated when on our way home some of us ran into a military truck with about four or five men inside along with two armed military guards sitting on the tailboard away from the men whom they were eyeing. We were convinced these were captured *maquisards* on their way to be interrogated and detained.

Tales about these maquisards were flames devouring the human brush. Parents warned their children about going out alone, especially into the neighbouring bushes, even those with patches of farmland. It was always a fresh scare to hear even of one more *maquisard* arrested. We heard of other legendary political characters like Kale, Mbile, Egbe, Ajebe-Sone, Kemcha, Motombi Woleta, and Abendong who, according to rumours, was mistakenly assassinated instead of

Foncha; we heard of Ntumazah, who was said to be one of the most mystical of all in the West Cameroon. His name alone struck a certain chord of awe and the supernatural for there were numerous stories about him, which gave people to understand that he could do and undo. However, I am convinced these were all myths that developed after these figures did that which many considered virtually impossible by managing to escape into exile after Ahidjo's government banned their beloved political party. We heard there were people who would see Ntum, as Ntumazah was fondly referred to by his admirers, driving a car along the straight street between the Bamenda Provincial hospital and his residence in Ntarinkon. The stories hold, however, that before he got to his neighbourhood where he would have be recognized with certainty, Ntumazah would disappear into thin air along with the vehicle he was driving. We heard of other characters with equally dreadful potentials from East Cameroon. We heard of Um Nyobe, Ouandie, and others. We heard of how the government was searching for these "terrorists" in vain. They could appear and disappear, the stories continued; some could even fly. We believed easily because of other similar tales we had heard of mysterious escapes by condemned criminals just as they were about to be executed.

There was in Buea, in those days, the story of a condemned criminal who just before they hanged him, they asked if he had any last request. They tell of how he said he wanted to eat a kite, but that he needed to touch the bird first before they killed it; it was his last wish, so they granted it. They gave him a kite; he tore it open, plugged out and swallowed the heart, plugged out the wings and attached each to either of his armpits and all of a sudden, the criminal flew away like a bird, cheating both death and the law. Many of such stories were circulating and, as children, we easily believed them, so Ntumazah appearing and disappearing in and from Cameroon, even though he was on exile, was not strange at all as these men and women standing against the government had powerful magical forces at their disposal, it was rumoured. The search for "terrorists" was the country's preoccupation at the time, and the authorities were doing everything to catch them.

Meanwhile, our family was settling down well in our new house in Bonaberi, Buea Town. School and my First Holy Communion classes were coming on fine and I was almost getting ready to be tested. If I passed, I was going in for First Holy Communion. I knew the prayers by rote and could not wait to begin taking communion on my tongue. With Frist Holy Communion, a necessary qualification, I could become an altar boy and begin accompanying priests onto the altar for Holy Mass. There were many of us kids with this dream and we all happened to be in the same school. I remember Raphael Jua, then the son of the Prime Minister of West Cameroon at one time, took Holy Communion with our group. There was Emmanuel Chila, Joseph Fonebi, Emmanuel Dohnji; Musa is the only name of another friend that I remember as school and classmates at RCM Buea Town. All these, added to our neighbourhood kids like Emmanuel Ewunkem, Nya, John Anyongo, Benson Nganda, Alfred Massa, Emmanuel and Gueni Elame, Gregory, Bernard, and Elizabeth kaba, Job, Zach, and Victoria Orji, Verseke and Enyoi Ekema, Pauline and Maggi Ndongmo, and Augustine the photographer's kid, peopled and affected one's life in many ways. As we all grew up, we met either in the neighbourhood, at school, or at church during and after Mass.

The chips seemed to be falling in place for my family, then it happened: Vince, my uncle, redirected his recalcitrance from my mother his oldest sister to my father—the head of the family. I do not know how it started, but on this day, we the children were outside playing in a small landing between the main building and the kitchen when all of a sudden Vince jumped out of my father's bedroom onto the landing below, which was in front of our kitchen. He swung around and started striking boxing stances, bouncing on his toes in the manner of Mohammed Ali, warming up in an obvious attempt to exchange blows with my father, the brother-in-law he had written letters to begging to be rescued from his socially depressing status back in Bamenda. He had dropped out of primary school since he could not pay his fees, and so he was only loafing around in the name of searching for any kind of unskilled job to do. In fact, at that moment, according to his letter, he was, while making a little money, spending his time running after cows as he guided them from the Bamenda Station through Banjah and Cow Streets to the abattoir. The abattoir was located on the left hand side of the road with Old Town on your right, close to the spot where today's Ayaba hotel is situated.

Accordingly, my father paid Vince's transport, which in those days was five hundred francs, and had Vince brought to him in Buea, at the Police Barracks where the family was at the time. My father, an excellent tailor himself, sat at a tailoring machine, sewed Vince's school uniforms, and had him registered at Roman Catholic Mission (RCM) Buea

Town. He was to be living with our family and attending primary school. In fact, Vince was treated like the member of our family that he was by right, given our culture—he was an in-law to my father—but here he was contrary to cultural expectations getting ready to fight an in-law old enough to play the role of a parent of his. My father did not take it lightly. When he came out after Vince and found him in a fighting stance like a boxer, my father gave a punch with his right fist and it landed on Vince's left arm. The latter staggered, stumbled, turned and ran away jumping down a shallow concrete wall and onto a newly prepared foundation, next to our house, which was still covered in grass. From there he stood looking back at us and wondering what my father was up to next since he did not immediately run after him. My father, really offended by this audacity and abuse of authority in his household, was determined to teach Vince a lesson he would never forget. Hence, my father went into his room but reemerged using the front main door into our apartment, which was on the opposite wall from which Vince was standing and darting furtive glances completely at a loss. My father sneaked round our building, out of Vince's view, into the neighbouring building next to which Vince was standing. Papa's idea was to emerge from behind and pounce on Vince. I was just six or seven years old at the time, a child of the family, who considered Vince himself just a few years older as another child of the household, and so it was only natural for me to side with Vince in the face of authority. I immediately signaled him by moving my hand in a manner indicative of the circular route my father had taken to emerge behind him. It was then it occurred to Vince what was going on; he turned just in time to see my father airborne towards him. Vince started, darted off and ran as fast as he could down the gentle but stony slope past Mr. Ndongmu's house on the right and Mammy Orji's to the left towards the Catholic Mission where the church stood. My father believed we were too young to have understood what was going on to the point of having given his little setup away and so did not even bother asking us who had given him away. He must have thought Vince was just lucky to have turned just when he was about to grab him. I keep wondering what my father would have done to me had he found out I am the one who gave him away to my uncle.

When Vince got down to the end of the street around where the building rented by Mr. Innocent, the Igbo Photographer, was on the left, and the new building on the right in which the late Mr. Neba, a primary school teacher from Bafut in the North West part of the country was living, he turned right and followed the short cut to Mount Mary Maternity. The path snakes through some old tombstones, descends and joins the main road leading to Mount Mary Maternity about fort–fifty feet down below. As he made his descent along that footpath, that was the last we saw of Vince. Until about a week later, Vince's destination remained a mystery to everyone in the household. My parents must have been worried about his whereabouts, but we never knew. Then my sister, Rita, and I, ran into Vince on our way to school one morning. He was still attending RCM Buea Town, but we were now attending RCM Buea Station. For some strange reason, my older sister who was in charge, decided we should avoid all short cuts to school on that day, and use the main road. Even then, there were at least two choices: we could go to school through the Buea Station neighbourhood. This meant walking from Buea Town following the main motorable road that meandered past then Basel Mission School, the police station, down past the Mobil Petrol Station, the Ministry of Education Building, heading down towards the Post Office and then to turn off to our school on the right, some distance away from the road. On the other hand, we could leave our house, go down to RCM Buea Town campus, walk past through it towards Lower Farms, across the motorable road where Kebila was killed, go past Mr. Lebaga's house and his Globus Shop, through the post office, down across our school's main field and up to the school. We took the latter route, and by the time we got to Lower Farms Prison fence, where a corm mill stood screaming in defiance of the number of bags of corn that was being poured into it, we ran into Vince who looked so emaciated Rita, without even thinking, offered him our food meant for our lunch break at school. Vince gobbled down some fried plantains, eggs, and scoops of beans. If he thanked us, I cannot remember, but we were glad to have fed him. We rushed off afraid of being late for school. It had not occurred to me to ask where he was living, and I cannot remember Rita asking either.

4

About a week had gone by when my father asked me to accompany him on a walk. It was not until we got to the Police Barracks where we used to live, a wonderful opportunity for me to see some old faces again, that I guessed where we were going. Together we visited Mr. Gregory Njawe, our former neighbor in Line 2 of Old Barracks, and there we met Vince doing the dishes. I assumed Mr. Njawe must have informed my father at work that Vince was with him and they had hatched the plan for Mr. Njawe to have him at home on this date and at a particular time. Vince, however, did not look startled by our arrival; he went on doing his dishes. Mr. Njawe must have told him he was expecting us; otherwise, Vince would have been frightened or at least surprised to see us. I cannot now remember what conversation transpired between my father and Mr. Njawe, but Vince never returned home. My father was wise and knew Vince, with his puckish ways, would bring problems into the family before long, and so at the onset of arguments now directed at him and no longer my mother, my father decided Vince had to go. I was only to meet him some years later in Victoria where I found him living with his nouveau riche maternal uncle.

At school, meanwhile, we worked, ate, played and learned as the days came and went, celebrating different church and government feast days. Above all the government feast days was "Umpire Day," as we called it, an aberration of "Empire Day." It was a day we celebrated with a lot of pomp. There was a march pass, and then schoolchildren were expected to feast on rice and stew prepared and supplied us at school. Our teachers simply asked us on the day before "Umpire Day" to come to school with a dish that had a cover. There was hardly any effective teaching or learning on that day. The school authorities shared food to thousands of children of the British Empire and we ate and ate, celebrating something about which we understood little. All we knew as children was that it had to do with belonging to the Queen of England we were told. This was the time in life one was also struggling to understand the difference between "Infants One" and "Standard One"; it was said that one was a higher grade than the other. We were learning about snow, black sheep, wool, wolf, and "Shokolokobangoshey," another term that was bandied around by senior pupils because it was in their Oxford Reader but which meant nothing to us. Then talk about shillings and pence started dying out and in their place we heard of francs. For quite a while as time went by, we kept stumbling on strange coins at home only to learn they were of the currency we used under the Queen.

Life seemed to be good; in fact, West Cameroon was a thriving society. Everything seemed to be working well for the people. Because there was respect for fellow citizens, respect for uniformed officers and the law, serious crime was virtually absent, and so there was a sense of security. When anything came up within the judiciary and legal system, it was immediately dealt with and appropriately too. We heard so much about the effectiveness of the dreaded Criminal Investigation Department (CID) police officers. There was talk of how at a crime scene these men and women would arrive and somehow retrieve the criminal's fingerprints from the scene and then with time they would use these prints to catch the criminal. I remember it was also the practice at the time, to give awards to police officers for a job well done. Sometime in 1963 or 64, my father was awarded a certificate and a cash prize of one thousand francs for distinguished police service; I think he helped solve a crime or something to that effect. We heard members of the CID unit were well trained, some as far away as the respected Scotland Yard. Virtually no crime was unsolved and the culprits brought before a magistrate without any waste of time where they were tried and immediately sentenced. I remember a neighbor of ours who was sentenced to twenty years imprisonment for forgery. What an embarrassment it was to see this once reasonably well to do and respected member of society in a convict's uniform, marching in a single file and stopping by his house when they worked nearby. Yes, less dangerous prisoners were always taken into town from time to time for manual labour such as trimming the lawns of government buildings, moulding of bricks and even construction work. A warder was always seen at the tail end of the file as they were guided to and from their destination. Because of their white outfit, people called them members of "White College," a euphemism for prison, of course.

We grew up learning the laws of the land from our parents. They told us what we could not do: "Do not tell lies for a liar is a thief; you can't steal, it's against the law; no bribery and corruption; you cannot destroy government property; a cheque is a legal tender, so if you must issue one, make sure there is money in the bank else you will go to jail." The economy, meanwhile, was thriving. There were richly equipped stores in Buea, most of which were owned by

Nigerians who had immigrated into Cameroon because of the Nigerian-Biafran war. There was Moody Brothers' Store, there was Family Store, and many others though smaller, along with richly supplied stalls selling so many different items. It was always fun running from Bonaberi quarters up into town—the shopping area—into Moody Brothers' Store to buy my father's favorite brand of batteries then—Nivico—for his small Philip's transistor radio to which we were always glued listening to Congo music and other radio broadcasts. Then there was Globus shop, a supermarket by our local standards in those days, owned by Mr. Lebaga. Globus was located across from Clerks' Quarters and the Police Barracks. You could find almost anything in Globus. In a one-car garage attached to one end of Globus, a huge Pontiac car was permanently parked. The story about this broad and equally long car, typical of the United States in the sixties and seventies, was that it had been banned off the road by the president of the country at the time, Ahmadou Ahidjo, because it was as big as the president's car. How sad it was for us to see this beautiful car permanently parked and never driven. We thought the president had to be a monster to do this to a compatriot. It was much later on in my life when it occurred to me that the car could have been grounded because there were no parts available for servicing it, and so after breaking down it was parked there with the hopes that somebody traveling to the US would be able to bring back the much-needed parts. There was nobody to confirm my suspicion in any case.

As the days came and went, we—my family and I—felt quite at home in our new surroundings in Bonaberi, Buea, and before long we got used to the families in the neighbourhood, especially the children, as we were growing up. There was Mammy Orji, the distinguished Igbo matriarch who was managing a small provision store and Off-license in the neighbourhood while frying and selling *poff-poff* from time to time. She was a mother to every child in the neighbourhood but always too busy to listen to our stories. She became such a mother because of her own children who were exemplary in the way they behaved themselves and related to others respectfully. The result was that Mammy Orji's children won the respect, friendship, and approval of most if not all of the neighbourhood kids and their parents. We knew they were Igbo, but it meant nothing to us, as we never looked at them as foreigners. At the time, there was no such vocabulary in our heads as children. We saw ourselves as kids just growing up and belonging to the same neighbourhood. There was the oldest of all Mammy Orji's children, a handsome young student then at Bishop Rogan's College, Buea; his name was Leonard, I think, but we called him "Brother Leo" for short. The "Brother" epithet in front of his name was just a sign of respect as we were brought up never to call an older sibling by his or her name, let alone someone who was already in college. Leo was too far out of our league and so all we could do was look up to him as the big brother and role model that he was. Our dream, which we considered far-fetched, was to go to college (as secondary schools were called in those days), like him. Leo's deportment made us want to go to "college" badly. He was neat, calm, quiet, and gentle even in the way he walked—a total gentleman.

The next Orji child was a decent young woman, somewhat fair in complexion, by name of Victoria if my mind is not failing me already. I cannot remember her name very well because of how she carried herself within a certain distance away from the rest of us, the boys; it was not arrogance but courteousness, decorum on her part I was convinced. Consequently, we just knew she existed but we never bothered ourselves about her. When we saw her, we exchanged brief greetings and that was it as she was also always busy by her mother "doing what women do," we thought. Then suddenly she was nowhere to be found for a while and so we asked after her only to hear she too had gone to college. Now we started asking what college was all about, and what one had to do to get there. May be the Orji kids knew a lot more about these things at the time since they already had a sibling in college; for me, it was a whole new thing.

It was about the same time that my only role model in terms of an older brother—Benson Nganda—left for St. Joseph's College, Sasse, Buea. I was devastated. I could not imagine life without this friend who had virtually become a brother to me. Benson Nganda was a Bakweri kid, but it never mattered that I was a Bamenda boy, that is if any such concepts existed at the time, or "graffi" as they would call me today. The door to my parents' home was open twenty-four hours seven days a week to Doctor as we fondly referred to Benson, and so was their home to me. Benson was last but one and so all the members of his family got used to me and there was no secret in that family that I did not know; how I loved them. There was their mother, the materfamilias, Yaya as we fondly called her; there was the oldest sister, Sister Esther, who was married and lived somewhere in Tiko at the time and only visited us from time to time, then after a while, as her own children started growing bigger and older, they too started visiting their aunts and grandmother. Then there was Sister Grace, Brother Emmanuel, and then Sister Ebenye aka Iya, an incredibly beautiful woman, then Benson, and lastly Christine whom we knew as Nainè. Their father had passed on earlier before I got to know them, and all I ever saw of him was a picture of him lying in state. We were family, and I spent virtually all of my spare time with Benson who was the greatest storyteller I had ever encountered. He was a complete gentleman with an ever-ready smile that rose to his face with the slightest excitement. I cannot remember ever seeing Benson upset; else, he kept it from me. He would narrate different movies he had watched for our entertainment at dusk until one would think one was in Potokri's cinema live. Benson would tell every step, produce every sound, and imitate the galloping of horses with keen details, his body jerking back and forth, as if he was actually on a horse instead of some low fireside stool; this was entertainment extraordinaire for me. I never wanted to be separated from this young man. Indeed, Benson could tell stories, and so much of what I knew growing up as a kid was thanks to him.

Benson taught me how to use the oil-seal of a huge truck as my childhood ride for work and play. After we located one of those rare big oil-seals with a thick rubber on the inside and all round the inner circumference of the seal, we hunted for one of those metal pieces branching off from the central rod and handle of an umbrella. We curved one end as the handle and then curved the other end such that it was used in guiding and directing the oil seal as it rolled on the ground. One had to be alert and adjust one's speed according to how fast one was pushing the seal on the ground. The oil seal, without its rubber lining, produced a kind of loud screeching noise that was only tolerated because of the pleasure one got rolling the seal around. The oil seal with the rubber lining still attached was ideal as it rolled around with a certain "thud" sound instead. We can compare the difference to the sound one hears with the banging shot of the door of much cheaper car and say that of a Mercedes Benz or similar quality car.

Benson would set up obstacles for us to try to beat without losing control of the wheel. It was not to tip on its side either; if it did then, it was the other person's turn to try. I used this wheel for play. I also used it to rush to and from places when running errands for my parents. Whereas my father understood that it helped me run errands in a timely manner, my mother just hated the wheel and the fact that it gave me the opportunity to play it seemed to me. I am at a loss explaining her hatred for the wheel even until today because it was not like Mom did not want to see me playing, no! In fact, she enjoyed watching me play, especially football, so I never was able to figure out what her problem was with my wheel, which I considered to be my ride. Accordingly, whenever she had the chance, she hid my wheel away from me or just threw it away altogether. I never knew my mother was responsible for the sudden disappearance of my wheel. To me, my wheel had just disappeared; I would stay without one until I was lucky to stumble on one washed down the street by floodwater due to a heavy downpour, and then the cycle would begin all over again. I would enjoy my ride until an opportunity presented itself for my mom to dispose of it again.

With Benson Nganda gone, I was determined to go to college too, but it had to be Bishop Rogan's College as my father hoped I could become a priest someday. Colleges were indeed far beyond the dreams of primary school kids. In every way, one could tell that going to college was a big deal: foremost was the fact that the students lived on campus away from their parents and only came home on occasions, first, during the mid-term break, which primary school kids did not have, and then on holidays like the rest of the national school system. The mid-term break made those of us in primary schools to understand that college students were above us. Whenever they were on mid-term break, we still had to be going to school for we had no such break. We heard from them about the good meals they had, and it was obvious because of how tall they suddenly became and how much they could easily wolf down only after a term in college. They even had eggs served them on Sundays; this was incredible. The name of the different subjects they studied just plain baffled us: Chemistry, Biology, Anatomy, Physics and so on. Their uniforms were brilliant white shirts and blue pairs of trousers unlike our pairs of shorts in elementary school. The students of Saint Joseph's College, Sasse, even had ties to go with their sparkling white shirts on special occasions, and then there was that blue long sleeve sweater edged with two yellow lines. To crown everything, they called those teaching them "Masters," unlike in primary school where we used the word "teacher." Their parents also gave them money to spend at will which they called pocket allowances. How we admired secondary school students and longed to be in their shoes.

I knew Leo Orji was in Bishop Rogan's College, the other younger Orjis were thinking of Bishop Rogan's College too, and we were great friends having virtually grown up together. There was Zach Orji who came after their sister, a quiet young man who spoke only when it was necessary for him to speak. He smiled occasionally, but I cannot now recall the things that made Zach smile, not to say laugh. He was a quiet person. I got the impression he was always present just to protect Job as he would look at one in a way that said it all if one rubbed in on Job the wrong way. The last of the Orjis was Job; in many ways like the older brother, Zach, and both very smart kids. Together we grew up in Buea town as pupils of RCM Buea Town, and then we became altar boys in the church of St. Anthony. We served Mass for priests like the Late Anthony Van De Vlugt, Late Alphonsus Ter Beke, Late Ivo Ndichia, Pius Awah, Francis Lysinge and Late Paul Vedzekov. The last three became Bishops of Buea, Mamfe, and the Archbishop of Bamenda respectively; of course, there was Bishop Julius Peeters at whose Masses we also assisted but on rare occasions since we were very young and mostly older boys from Bishop Rogan's College served during his Masses. He was the one who confirmed us as Catholic Christians. He sat there at the foot of the altar and we walked up to him in our bright white confirmation outfits in a single file. He blessed us, one after the other, gave a few words of encouragement, I believe, for we could not quite get his accent, and then a little pat on the jaw. It became routine, such that I grew up thinking the pat at the end of the confirmation ritual was a necessary part of the procedure. I was therefore disappointed in later years to see Bishops who did not give that gentle pat, then it dawned on me it was just a habit of Bishop Peeters' and not a necessary part of the sacrament.

Another family that still stands out in my mind in the neighbourhood was the Ndongmo family. Mr. Ndongmo had two beautiful girls I still remember: Pauline and Maggi, I think. Pauline's name I am certain about as we both went to RCM Buea Town, but I think Maggi was ahead of us in school; she was already in Okoyong too while we tried to bring our elementary school years to a close. Their home was a little further away from the road and so it was hard to get to them especially without a boy being in the family as we were growing up. Occasionally, however, we stumbled on them coming from school or somewhere from the mission area. The family was so united it was much later on in life I learned that Mr. Ndongmo was just the eldest son in the family, but he took so much care of his siblings that one thought he was their father. Those, however, were the days when there was hierarchy in the family; those were the days when younger siblings respected the older ones accordingly, who then helped their parents in bringing up their younger siblings; not today with its woes of disrespect, decadence, and debauchery resulting mainly from the influence of alien values now destroying Africa's noble ways.

Then there was Mr. Innocent, the Photographer, another Igbo man, in "last town" as his location was called. His was the last house before the bushes that separated the Catholic mission estate from the rest of the town. Mr. Innocent had a son, Augustine, who was one of us, but I cannot recall the secondary school he went to; maybe he returned to Nigeria sooner than the rest. Buea was alive and we were happy children growing up as a people without all these ridiculous divisions now characterizing the nation: "anglo," "frog," "enemies in the house," "come-no-go," "graffi," "sawa," and so on. When a person is considered an alien in his own fatherland and by his own people, then it becomes obvious the degree of lawlessness that is prevailing. How sad is it that this is all the progress we have made after all these decades? Yes, "Vikuma" had been heard of as a political slogan standing for "Victoria Kumba Mamfe" and a song about Bakweri people refusing to join the military because of *kwacoco*. Yet, there was nothing as insulting and divisive between West Cameroonians like today's "Come-no-go," "graffi," "Bamenda come down," or "Bagili," derogatory terms used by the South Westerner for the North Westerner, as opposed to the latter's very recent "Nkwah," for the South Westerner. Accordingly, while growing up, we flourished completely unaware of who was "graffi," who Bakweri or who Biafra: we were kids growing up, and life was fun and we loved it. We only looked forward to playing different games at school during recess, serving during daily and especially weekend Masses, cleaning up church paraphernalia on Saturday mornings, and going to out-stations. Some of the outstations we visited were places like Middle Farm prison, Bokwaongo, Bulu, Muea and even as far as Victoria when Fr. Anthony felt like some fresh breeze from the sea after we left Bulu or one of those out-stations in the Mile 17 area and therefore closer to Victoria.

Beyond the capital city of Buea, there was Victoria the economic heartthrob of West Cameroon. My first trip ever to Victoria was a most remarkable experience for me. I had just returned from the Buea GRA (Government Residential Area) where I had spent a week with family friends, the Ntunes, during which week I became very used to cars as we went shopping in a car, and went to Mass on Sunday in a car. Later on in the day on which I was supposed to return home—Sunday afternoon—this beautiful older daughter of my host's drove me back home in Town. When she left, my father who had a trip to visit his maternal uncle, Pa Joe, in Victoria scheduled, asked if I wanted to come along. I always loved going around with my father because as we walked he constantly seized the opportunity to pass on to me valuable life lessons which he had learned, like the need to be educated, the need to be humble and to enjoy being of service to people. He would instruct me always to tell the truth and then die if that was what it entailed, rather than to tell a lie. He would warn me against smoking and drinking before going on to talk about the value and strength of prayer as we walked to our destination; his favourite prayer book: *St Anthony's Treasury*. One of his illustrations of the power of prayer, which I really enjoyed listening to, was how he misplaced his Miraculous Medal upon exiting the Catholic Church at Bota by the sea, only to miraculously hoe it out of the ground in Buea while farming. This, of course, was after a novena to St. Anthony whose dedicated devotee he was, St Anthony the saint reputed for helping people find misplaced things. Yes, I remember my father's *St. Anthony's Treasury* prayer book being so worn from use.

My father and I left the house and walked to the taxi park up the main street entering Buea Town, where we boarded a taxi for Victoria; we were visiting Uncle Joe, my paternal grandmother's brother who worked for the CDC (Cameroon Development Corporation) and lived in the Bota camp. These camps were made up of tiny apartments—a small parlour and an equally small bedroom—which were occupied by families as large as six or even ten in number. With all the money generated for decades for the CDC by these hard working families, these cubicles they occupy have never been refurbished in anyway, let alone redesigned when the authorities realized that the families were beginning to be bigger than anticipated. One cannot help wondering then, if there was any kind of planning or feasibility studies done before these camp houses were built this way. A sane leadership, or, to be fair, one with its citizens at heart, would have built newer and slightly bigger camp-buildings for workers with wives and children, and have these older worn out camps refurbished for bachelors and smaller families. However, this is such a far-fetched concept to the executives of this corporation and many others like this in Cameroon; after all, they have beautiful bungalows for themselves with equally affluent facilities strictly for management.

About an hour had gone by when my father and I alighted from the taxi that had brought us from Buea around the Gardens neighbourhood in Victoria and started walking towards our destination. As we walked down the gentle slope, around the entrance to the zoo, approaching the Bota Oil Mill, my father pointed at the sea in the distance, but all I could see was the horizon or that is what I thought it was.

"Where is it Father?" I asked curiously.

"There, follow my finger," my father said, pointing in the direction of the ocean.

"I am not seeing anything."

"There, look at those trees," he said, pointing at one of the islands in the middle of the sea "they are right in the water."

I could see the trees, but the sea was the same colour as the horizon, so I could not get the picture my father wanted me to get.

"Don't worry, we'll be there soon."

"Okay," I answered as I walked proudly by father, with my hand in his, taking in the beauty of the scene all around me.

My father navigated his way through neatly kept driveways hedged by well-trimmed flowers, until we emerged right in front of the Bota Catholic Church by the sea. It was my very first encounter with the ocean, and so I found myself hopping from stone to stone on the rather stony shore by the church. My father urged me to and I tasted the water to confirm its salty quality about which he had talked to me earlier on. I was overwhelmed by what came across as a rather well programmed set of events by nature: I watched the sea waves rolling towards the shore as if some invisible giant house cleaner was folding the sheets of an incredibly large bed. Alas the powerful volume of waves, upon getting to the shore, would smash against rocks in some areas and at others right against man-made walls and then disintegrate into foams with an effervescent effect as it rolled back head-on into another powerful wave surging towards the shore. The walls seemed to hold back the waves with an assured confidence they could go on forever as the waves splashed with a certain gentle ferocity that sent showers into the air and the surrounding environment. The sizes of the two ships berthed in the ocean away in the distance were baffling. I could see the lighters apparently gliding slowly back and forth the ships. My father explained that because of the rocks by the shore, the ships could not get any closer than they were already, and so they use the lighters to transport cargo from the ships to the shore where they are stored; the rhythm was enchanting and held me spellbound. My father talked to me about the deep seaport being natural as opposed to another one in a much bigger city called Douala in the French speaking part of the country. The bad thing with that port, my father pointed out, is that it was up a river and the bottom filled with mud from time to time and so the country, for a huge sum, got white men to come and dig it further down for the ships to be able to come close to the wharf.

"So why don't all the ships just come here?" I asked, looking up at my father and waiting for him to explain.

"That is a very good question," my father replied, looking at me with curiosity in his eyes.

"There are many reasons which you would not understand if I gave them to you now, but I am sure as you grow up you will be able to figure these things out yourself. For now, just know that the big people in Yaounde do not want it."

"Yaounde? Where is Yaounde? But why do the big people not want it?"

"You see, that's what I meant when I told you, you would not understand. You are still too young to understand these things. Yaounde is our capital city."

"What is capital city, Father?"

"Capital city means the city where the president is living."

"Okay!" I answered satisfied.

"You know who the president is right?

"Ahidjo?" I replied questioningly.

"That's good."

I could not believe the ships could come and line up against a wall, but my father insisted that they did. Together my father and I sat there watching the sea and sharing stories and questions and answers until my father suggested it was time for us to go find Uncle Joe.

Uncle Joe was very glad to see me. It felt strange when my father told me Uncle Joe was his uncle. I could not fathom my father having an uncle; I thought he was too big to have any other person that could make him look like or come across like a child; an uncle? Yet there he was before us: a very tall man, a typical Bali breed, with a gentle smile. He was glad to see me, and said so much in Mungaka that I can barely remember; it was all about praise for me, and how grown up I was compared to when he last saw me when he visited us in Buea. I could remember the visit vaguely. He was, at the time, still planning his wedding to his wife, Ma Mary. At Uncle Joe's, we ate, drank, and then he and my father talked and talked. When we left Uncle Joe's house later on in the day, my father took me to see the animals at the Victoria Zoo. What an experience that was for me. For the first time I saw a lion, an elephant, the snakes, the crocodiles and the notoriously acrobatic and equally noisy and boisterous monkeys. Victoria, with all these resources—the botanical gardens, the sea, the zoo, the river, the hotels, the huge shops, was unparalleled to me. In me, I wished we were living in Victoria instead of Buea.

The sun was already setting when we boarded another taxi at Half Mile Victoria on our way back to Buea. At Mile 17, Buea Road, as was the practice, the driver stopped briefly for passengers to buy roasted corn, sugarcane or whatever fruits they needed. I could not wait to get home and sink my teeth into the sugarcane. In any case, as if reading my thoughts, my father pacified me with fresh roasted corn at which I nibbled until we got off the taxi in Buea Town. About an hour later, when we walked into our home, I wanted to go to sleep right away; it had been one of the best weeks in my entire life. As I ate my dinner, my mother listened to my stories about my trip to Victoria and my encounter with the ocean and later on with Uncle Joe and his family. I cannot remember how I got into bed that day; I must have slept while eating and my father carried me off and tucked me into bed.

5

The frequency of Ahidjo's visits to West Cameroon was increasing greatly as he struggled to impress and at once impose himself on Southern Cameroonian politicians by pitting them against each other. The nation was virtually in a state of emergency to make movement for the escaping UPCists difficult. The true heroes were fighting against foreign control over Cameroon politics, for which reason they branded them *maquisards* so as to hunt them down and kill them. Not only the so-called *maquisards* suffered; the entire population suffered greatly as movement was zealously controlled and restricted. Although they said it was from one administrative division to another, the truth is citizens could not move freely from one main town to another. To do this, the potential traveler had, in advance, to go to a government official like a District Officer (DO), to get permission to go across what were virtually arbitrary boundaries or political borders since the police were everywhere. The potential traveler applied for a pass known in French as the "Laissez Passer." The said official could deny the subject the right to travel for some flimsy reason. Since the so-called *maquisards* could not go to request this document without being arrested, travelling via the main roads and by vehicle or means of public transport was out, which complicated matters for them. The said "Laissez Passer" was to be presented each time a uniform officer asked for it at one of the numerous checkpoints that now littered the highways between major towns. There were numerous sporadic checkpoints along all the roads between major towns and cities, with uncouth gendarmes demanding documents from passengers in a most disrespectful manner. West Cameroonians were wondering what was happening to them; they were not used to having disrespectful law officers harassing them; they were used to a friendly police force that was there to protect them. It was obvious the administrative landscape was changing, yet little did Southern Cameroonians, now called West Cameroonians, know their disturbing and overwhelming experience was only a prelude to the abuse of power they would soon experience as a permanent part of their lives because of their newfound relationship with la République. Cameroon was never to give up the state of emergency mentality nurtured at this time in the nation's history, with poorly trained uniformed officers hassling citizens on a permanent basis for no good reason other than the need to be bribed for being the nuisance they were. They only intensified the nature of their badgering when decades after a certain Paul Biya became president and imposed a state of emergency on the people of Bamenda, one of several parts of the country where the people know who they are, what they want and expect from their leaders, and are not ashamed of their identity.

Besides the political turbulence conjured into existence in West Cameroon as Ahidjo manipulated the population in an effort to find out those who could work with him from a subservient position, all else in West Cameroon was thriving: from Lido Bar in Kumba, a life band produced long lasting records that kept one abreast with the tide of events. There was Johnny Tezano's "Tiko Drink Kumba Drunk" track, then there was "Competition for Kumba," there was another track "Powercam," celebrating the coming of electricity into Bamenda, Bamenda, which was the home of West Cameroons Santa Coffee Estate, which grew, processed, and distributed high grade coffee all over West Cameroon and beyond in the sixties. Equally distinguished, was the Bali Modern Jazz Orchestra with tracks that were blaring forth from every loudspeaker one could find in those days. Life was good; there was every indication that West Cameroon was a thriving community: a disciplined police force that respected the public and so was esteemed in return and a society largely free of crime as criminals were swiftly tried and immediately punished. Nobody was above the law, such that even uniformed officers who abused the law or blundered in any other manner considered serious and unbefitting of officers of the law were immediately tried and sentenced accordingly.

Health wise, there were sanitation officers who worked for the local councils, whose duty it was to visit homes to ascertain they met council standards for cleanliness. The hospitals were not only well equipped with distinguished nurses' aides, nurses, nursing sisters, and doctors, they also handed out free medication; one only had to provide the bottle and one's medications were quickly dispensed free of charge. Consequently, some people became self-employed and were providing bottles to patients for a token fee. The consultation route was clearly mapped out and easy to follow. A patient arrived the hospital and registered through an official sitting in a room and attending to patients through an open window. It was usually a woman at this post; she would stamp a consultation card with the hospital's seal before handing it out to the patient for a token fee. The patient would then proceed when it was his or her turn to another official who then wrote the date of consultation on the card, along with the patient's personal information: address, date of birth, marital status and so on. The patient was then shown where to sit in line on benches that snaked around an opening to accommodate the dozens of patients waiting to consult. With every patient seen by the nurses on duty, room opened at the tail end of the wooden snake as the occupants dragged their butts forward to occupy the space that had just been evacuated at the front of the cue. Slowly but surely the patients consulted. Those whose cases were considered more serious or complicated than the almost routine malaria, cough, and fever, were sent to another queue at the end of which they consulted a doctor. The trend, however, was that having done with consultation, one moved over to the pharmacy to join another line which crawled forward at the same spasmodic pace triggered by the departure of one more patient at the end of the line until one got one's medication.

The hospital then was made up of long zinc buildings that looked oval, but with one-half of the "O" shape apparently under the ground. The buildings were no different from those of the new neighbouring camp with a high gate at the top of which was written "Gendarmerie Nationale," a new paramilitary group that was just surfacing in West Cameroon. At the gate was always a sentry with a semi-automatic rifle in his hand, and a revolver dangling from a belt around his waist. Nobody seemed to know what the role of these people speaking French was; we heard they were from East Cameroon, and so we could not help questioning their reasons for carrying guns since all we were used to, were police officers with truncheons when they were armed.

Socially, Buea had a lot to offer: there were bars and hotels along Long Street, Small Soppo, Bokwaongo, as well as in Buea Town and Great Soppo, that catered for the social life of the people and those visiting. At night especially, one could hear life bands blaring forth the latest music, with men and women in search of fun milling about. There was Mammy Christina's bar in Buea Town and Hotel Memoz in Long Street, Great Soppo that distinguished themselves with musicians from the Congo. On the other hand, I remember the traditional wrestling bouts—*palapala*—held once a week, I think, on an open arena that doubled for a football field far within the Bakweri village, as the area way behind the council office up there in the hill was called. Brave young men from different villages surrounding Buea—Bokwai, Bulu, Bwasa, Bonakanda, Bokwaongo, Bova, and the rest—would assemble in different camps on different weeks, around the wrestling arena, themselves surrounded by a rumbling crowd of the young and the old alike, boys, girls, men, women, all cheering. From time to time a section of the crowd danced in and out of the arena guided by the gyrating tunes from different drums played by aged but skilled drummers. Beads of sweat could be seen shimmering and glistening on their bodies when the sun managed to hit them through the holes in the thick boughs of a number of trees under which they were sitting.

With a loincloth strapped firmly around his waist, a young and well-built wrestler would emerge from his team and dance round the arena daring the opposing village for that week if they could produce a befitting opponent. After a while, the challenged village would decide on a worthy opponent who would accept the challenge and step out moving to the rhythm of the drums that were still being skillfully attacked by the musicians. Both wrestlers would continue sizing each other while closing in onto the center of the arena. Upon a signal from the umpire, the two would charge into each other hoping to tilt the advantage the one in his favour and the other in his. The goal was to put the opponent's back on the ground. The jousting of powerfully muscled arms would continue, some coming with powerful open-handed slaps to the opponent's shoulder blade in the hope of causing him to lose his balance so the aggressor would charge in and flip the opponent over. This went on until one wrestler would emerge as the winner, or until the bout was declared a draw. In either case, supporters from the villages would charge into the arena and carry their wrestler shoulder high dancing and celebrating the win or draw. Losers just left the arena quietly conceding to the other's superiority, which they hoped to challenge sometime in the future.

These wrestling bouts were taken so seriously such that there were stories about the strategic role played by the supernatural during the bouts. One would hear comments like "that young man's juju is the gorilla. You see those powerful arms and chest like those of a gorilla, if he should succeed in gripping his opponent, that's all; he will slam him to the ground." There were others whose "juju," it was alleged, had to do with the tiger, the elephant and so on. These wrestling bouts brought life to Buea where especially The Buea Mountain Hotel was the ultimate accommodation resort that catered for the needs of distinguished visitors to West Cameroon's political capital. Situated at the foot of Mount Cameroon, the weather was usually foggy and wet during the rainy season, with a refreshing pleasantness during the dry season. Its proximity to the economic capital of Victoria made it an ideal facility, a cocoon from which adventurers emerged for a brief spell in Victoria before quickly retreating to base.

Victoria was unparalleled in West Cameroon it would seem to me. Not even Kumba aka K-Town, with all its popular neighbourhoods like Fiango and Hausa Quarter to name a few, along with the live music that characterized and buoyed social life in this wonderful city, or Tiko with its famous airport and popular Airport Hotel could reduce Victoria to second place. Tiko and Kumba were extraordinarily vivacious cities rivaling each other virtually, even as the record "Tiko Drink Kumba Drunk" authenticated, yet Victoria aka Va., was a city in a class of its own. The truth though is that each town in West Cameroon was unique, with distinguishing flavours heightened by the geography, the people, and their culture. Victoria was a port city with its southern periphery incessantly splashed by the powerful waves of the Atlantic Ocean that charged inland in rolls only to crash against the jutting rocks at one point, or against fabricated retaining walls at another. Because of the sea, the port, the visiting ships, and their sailors, businesses of all sorts bloomed to gratify the large number of guests arriving from all over West and East Cameroon, overseas even. There was Park Hotel Miramar, Atlantic Beach Hotel, and Bay Saloon Hotels all with extraordinary accommodations and entertainment for tourists. The life band in Bay Saloon, especially, rocked Victoria by night, and so did the discothèques in the other nightclubs like Crystal

Garden, which were usually attached to these beautiful coastline hotels.

Most people, especially visitors, spent their days in Victoria shopping in the many different shopping centers that used to decorate the streets of Victoria. There was R & W King, Emen Textiles, Alliance, Glamour, Presbook, and Printania to name a few. There was even a Renault vehicle dealership in Victoria on the left on the way to Down Beach, just after the Centenary Stadium Roundabout, while Neba's Volvo dealership controlled Mutengene, a few miles away from the heart of Victoria. It was pure entertainment just watching the uniformed staff of these dealerships going around servicing vehicles, while in the display room stood one or two brand new Renault or Volvo cars.

Because of Printania's location by the sea, next to which stood the Alfred Saker Memorial, I used to love going into Printania, round about 4:00pm, to buy different brands of bar chocolate—Mambo and Tcha-tcha being my favourite at the time. I would emerge from the shop and sit by the Alfred Saker Memorial munching bar after bar of chocolate while watching the lighters from the Bota wharf burp on the surface of the ocean as they shuttled to and from the ships berthed in the distance. At the same time, my body, my face especially, was soothed by the powerful yet refreshing winds from the Atlantic Ocean. I enjoyed, above all, the water level climbing as the direction of the tide changed towards the land. To me, as a child growing up then, life seemed like a permanent vacation. If it was not this favorite pastime of mine, it was riding bicycles all over Botanical Gardens. For 500 FRS also, one rented a bicycle for the whole day from one of those Igbo businesspersons along the streets in Down

Beach without even submitting any kind of collateral, not even an identification paper of any sort. Beyond riding bicycles with those rich kids who lived in the premises of the Botanical Gardens and owned bicycles of their own, there was the zoo where I visited the animals. On the other hand, I sometimes spent time just strolling around the Botanical Gardens eating all kinds of fresh fruits, to which we had given local names. That fruits dangled from colorful trees, sometimes short and stout and sometimes towering, and found all over the garden. There was a fruit that we the children of the hour called "Bobi water." I cannot quite remember what the fruit looked like, but its rather peculiar name was stuck on my mind. All I recall was its brownish skin and the fact that it was extraordinarily succulent and a sweet milky-white liquid of some kind literally dripped down one's hands after one bit into it. Then there was "couluba," a grape-like fruit from a huge tree with an unusually rich bough, although its fruits dangled as singles and not in bunches like grapes. Picture yellow grapes hanging in singles all over a tree richly endowed with leaves and branches, and one has a clear picture of the "couluba" tree and its fruits. The fruit is usually green, then it begins turning yellowish as it gets ripe and ready for consumption. Its sour taste was outstanding and equally unique was its notoriety for "killing one's teeth" as we described the sensitive nature of one's teeth after eating "couluba." This effect was felt more when one parted one's lips and tried sucking in air through clamped teeth.

There were also cinemas in Victoria. Rivoli, somewhat the popular of the two, was situated between Gardens and Bota, and Rio Cinema was in New Town. My personal favorite for reasons of proximity and the straight route that got one to it was Rivoli. I would watch a movie on Sunday, become so involved such that I was left sad by the end of the show. It was as if I had two lives, but that which I lived during a movie, into which I steeped myself, was always a lot more fun but short-lived. I usually came to myself at the end of the movie as people were shoving into chairs and each other on their way out of the hall. It was as if a curtain was slowly moving or thinning away and bringing me back into a comparatively boring reality with rules to obey and other boring aspects of life to deal with. I always had a feeling of remorse at the end of a movie, but I also learned to accept and deal with it.

The Oil Mill at Bota was not only an economic asset, it was a teaching and touristic site: students and tourists witnessed the processing of a product from scratch to finish on excursions, the former as part of a Geography class and the latter, although it was a learning experience to them also, they did it mainly to be entertained. One was beckoned to the mill from the distance by the tantalizing smell of kernels cooking in the process of extracting kernel oil. In the premises there were little carts rolling to and from processing destinations with freshly harvested kernel fruits on the one hand, and those that had already succumbed to the oil extracting process from which *menyang*a, another locally popular kind of oil is extracted, and so on. Victoria, like West Cameroon as a whole, was a city with a purpose and a sense of direction. We were a proud people.

The facilities were functioning well because of the supply of affordable electricity. From a dam at Yoke, in Muyuka, electricity was generated and efficiently supplied all over West

Cameroon for next to nothing as opposed to the nightmare West Cameroonians are experiencing today in the form of high electricity bills and frequent blackouts. There were streetlights and they worked; they were turned on and off at specific hours by a conscientious worker. Water, on the other hand, was not a problem. There were public taps all over the place to which people who could not afford pipe borne water in their homes got water free. It is for this reason I was shocked when the first time, in 1977, I saw people in Bafoussam with public taps that had no faucets. Citizens had to have a green rubber tube that they brought from home. They would stick this tube into a funny little outlet from the main pipe sticking out of the ground, pull at the tube with their mouths and then quickly direct the flow into their containers. How unhygienic was it to syphon portable water for the family in this manner, I thought; it meant each time the bearer syphoned the water by sucking with his or her mouth, spittle went into the container with the first flow. "Disgusting!" I concluded. Today, we are close to this nauseous practice as the water cooperation now rations water in parts of West Cameroon.

Talk of water and one thinks of the fresh man-made spring that used to be located next to Limbe River under the district officer's residence, which was located up in the hill on the Centenary Stadium side of town. A pump pumped out cold, fresh, and pure water from under the earth, which people drank to refresh themselves after strolling around the Botanical Garden. Because of the "tim-tim" sound, the pump produced as it pumped up water from below, the pump earned the onomatopoeic name of Tim-tim. Instead of nursing this touristic treasure that refreshed tourists in the

Botanical Gardens, as would have been the case in any society with foresight, Tim-tim was instead disconnected. The idea, obviously, was to prevent people from fetching water from there should they try avoiding the exorbitant water bills imposed on the public by the succeeding French-backed water corporation, Société Nationale des Eaux du Cameroun (SNEC).

The soil in the coastal areas of West Cameroon is very fertile because of its volcanic nature some have pointed out, and so, as some West Cameroonians put it, all one has to do in these areas is turn over a stone and plant and whatever it is will flourish. As children, we used to join our neighbours, like the Kabas and the Ngandas in Bonaberi quarter in Buea Town, on trips to their farms. With the Kabas, we went to Bulu because of the fruit trees that were all over the farm; with the Ngandas, we went up the mountain in search of adventure more than for farming reasons. Up in the mountain with the Ngandas, we would fell a tree, chop it into logs which we carried back home for wood. I was always part of this just for the thrill and nothing else. My father used to buy wood from the forestry department in those days, and it would be supplied to our home. However, with our neighbours, the Ngandas, I used to enjoy the preparations for, and then the trip up the lower parts of the mountain.

On Friday evening, the eve of our frequent Saturday trips to the mountain for wood, we would prepare some *Kwa-coco bible*, cocoyam which is ground, laced with palm oil, richly spiced, tied and cooked in specially prepared leaves, which we would then re-heat in the morning before we left; it was to serve as our lunch up in the mountain. I could not understand how I got my father to permit me, then his only son, to go on a trip like this, which could easily turn dangerous. There were chances I could easily fall with a log of wood on my head along the sometimes slippery paths meandering up and down the mountain and hurting myself, or being bitten by a snake, or even attacked by some animal. It is either my father trusted my dear friend Benson Nganda so much or else he wanted me to experience life in a way that would toughen me because of what he himself had gone through. I later found out in life that it was both; my father trusted Benson and wanted me to experience things as I forged my own path in life. His very strong religious beliefs convinced him that a child born to live would live come what may. Many things were to happen later on in my life that convinced me of the appropriateness of my father's philosophy and worldview. The trip up the lower parts of the mountain was not easy for a nine-year-old kid, but thoughts of us relaxing after some work and devouring our delicious *kwa-coco* and washing it down with Champagne Soda, which was red in colour and sweet, kept me excited and interested all the way.

Most village neighbourhoods in Buea were fenced in, and so from our homes in Bonaberi, we walked for about half a mile, and then went in through the gate into fenced-in Bova. After walking for about a third of a mile across Bova, we got to the last gate across which one was officially on the mountain. Even before going through this gate, we stopped at one Mola's house; his fenced yard shared a wall with the mountain fence. His name is now faded from my mind. In this Mola's house, we would harvest some passion fruits, which we ate as we continued up the mountain. As we climbed up the mountain, I remember so many different thoughts crossing my mind. I wondered where all the animals were that we could climb up this far and not meet any. I remember Benson reassuring me once that if we waited where we were until it was about getting dark, we were sure to hear gorillas approaching. We were not stupid to try justifying this claim which Benson himself had only heard from some folks. How were we to deal with the gorillas if it turned out true?

I also used to wonder about the mythical figure stories claimed resided at the peak of the mountain, the *Efasa Moto*. Myths hold that the figure was part man-part woman, while others said it was part human and part rock. There were stories of points up the mountain beyond which one would not be able to find one's way back; of a sugar cane farm from which one could not bring back any. It was rumoured that one could eat all the sugar cane one felt like eating while up in the mountain, but as soon as one tried taking some away, one forgot the way out of the sugar cane farm.

Then we would make it to the farm, drop our lunch bags and begin weeding. We paused from time to time to chat, laugh, and scare each other because of the strange bird and animal sounds that sometimes pierced the surrounding silence. The cool breeze, even with the proximate towering trees, was always refreshing as it played on our faces and the leaves of nearby plants causing them to move fixedly in a particular fashion as if some invisible hand was doing it. Sometimes, and this was always reassuring, one could hear other farmers holding conversations across farms in loud voices, or someone using an axe to fell a tree, then the crashing of the tree would be heard. This was usually followed by loud ululations from the man with the axe as a reassuring sound that he was okay; else, someone was likely to think the crashing tree had hurt him.

At about 1:00pm, as we ate lunch, some of our group began felling a selected tree from which we were to cut logs in readiness for our return trip home. By 4:00pm, depending on how soon it got dark during a particular season, we would hack logs out of the felled trees, which we then carried home for firewood. The return trip was more tiring than our journey up the mountain, yet more exciting. With at least a log of wood precariously balanced on one's head, depending on one's size, we half-walked and half-ran down the slope in a single file with nobody wanting to be the one at the tail of the file for fear of some unknown mysterious force snatching one without the rest knowing. It was fun but dangerous because of how slippery the path down the slope could be at times, especially if it rained. Our goal was to make it through the gate separating Bova from the mountain before it got dark. Once through the gate, we would relax, confident we could no longer have any encounters with monkeys, chimpanzees, or mysterious forces because of the many human beings now milling around. We would then begin laughing at our fears, which now seemed foolish, childish, and baseless. We got home to a warm bath and then a meal, before heading off to bed after telling our experiences of the day to the rest of the family.

6

It was about this time in our lives, 1967/68, that we were cascaded by word about the ongoing Nigerian-Biafran war. I did not know who those fighting were, but we saw many and lived by so many refugees escaping from the war. It was equally a daily mantra over Radio Nigeria as it was announced repeatedly after a particular signature tune, "To keep Nigeria one is a task that must be done." On the Biafran side meanwhile, the mantra was "The price of liberty is internal vigilance, Biafra be vigilant!" Who did not know the inspiring voice of Okoko Ndem on Radio Biafra! The battle raged on, even as Ahidjo quietly went to work putting in place his master plan for Cameroon: he started by eliminating the federal system of government and replacing it with the United Republic of Cameroon. In hindsight, this was a major political victory for Ahidjo, a coup d'état in other words, and a landmark political tornado touchdown over the already established political institutions of West Cameroon. Yet this could not have happened without the complete or near total sterilization, at the very least, or annihilation in the extreme, of Ahidjo's political rivals and avowed opponents, especially those who belonged to the UPC. Most of them either were dead or already out of the country in exile, but a few were still on the run in West Cameroon. Enter the last phase of the political drama directed by Ahmadou Ahidjo: the arrest of Ernest Ouandie, Bishop Ndongmo and the rest. The Right Reverend man of God was accused of harbouring and assisting terrorists—Cameroonians who wanted their country,

East Cameroon, to engage a different political agenda than what France and Ahidjo had in place. Ahidjo, by this time, had succeeded in painting a terrible image of the Bamileke as a terroristic ethnic group. Their villages were constantly under attack by government troops, local and foreign alike, as Gaullists struggled for the successful installation of a puppet at the helm of Cameroon's affairs.

West Cameroon was now floundering almost without a sense of direction, given that the United Nations and Great Britain had transformed this territory and her citizens into pawns and political baits along different corridors of power. Great Britain, which was administering Southern Cameroons, then a United Nations protectorate, gave up her responsibility in a most shameful manner. It became obvious, especially with the passing of time that Britain did not care about what happened next to a people one would have loved to say she had once cared for, and who were a part of the British Empire directly or otherwise. However, how does one say this given Britain's rather irresponsible manner of abandoning Southern Cameroon without following the steps that Britain and the United Nations had put in place for the executing of this exercise? Unlike France, which, until of recent, was still a strong presence in the affairs of Cameroon, Britain never looked back to see how Southern Cameroons was fairing in a predicament into which they had been forced by Britain and the United Nations. Otherwise, why was Southern Cameroons compelled to gain her independence only by joining the Federal Republic of Nigeria or La République du Cameroun? After all, there are nations far smaller than Southern Cameroons existing on the continent of Africa today. Accordingly, the idea that Southern Cameroons would have been too small of a nation is irrelevant. The outcome is evidence leading to a conviction of a connivance at the level of the UN and Britain to dispose of Southern Cameroon as quickly as possible. Britain was very willing to oblige because she had underestimated Southern Cameroons' economic potentials and so did not want the future nation to depend on Her Majesty's Treasury for any kind of assistance. The implications are numerous even as now evidenced by newly declassified documents.

Meanwhile, Cameroon's Nelson Mandela, Albert Womah Mukong, was already savouring the woes of being a political prisoner. Whereas his peers quickly kept quiet—thereby betraying Southern Cameroons—to earn political positions from Ahidjo, Mukong, without fear, always said what he thought about the system even if it meant denouncing Ahidjo. Accordingly, Ahidjo had transferred Mukong from one political prison to another, but dreaded meeting Mukong in person. What a prophetic name, Mukong—the spear. Mukong fought for West Cameroon and the oppressed until his demise in 2004. To some he had become anathema, especially those West Cameroonians who fell for Ahidjo's political pacifiers. Some considered Mukong a loser for fighting for his people all his life, but to the majority, he remains a respected nationalist with a foresight with which nature had denied awarding virtually the rest of his age mates. This fact was already obvious from his days as a student at the University College of Ibadan where this altruist started suffering and fighting against the plight of Southern Cameroonians.

Meanwhile, the trial of Bishop Albert Ndongmo, Ernest Ouandie and the rest of the group went on. Even as kids, one could feel the tension in the air as the Ahidjo regime, which had already heavily victimized the Bamilekes, tried Bishop Ndongmo and his partners, all Bamileke men. Christians waited to see what Ahidjo, a Muslim head of state, was going to do with a Christian bishop. After all, it was clear the trial was a travesty: Ahmadou Ahidjo knew what he wanted the verdict to be. It has been reported that he declared in an interview: "Ndongmo, I despise him, I will not kill him but Ouandie, I respect him and I will kill him." Accordingly, in the wake of all the ado of a so-called trial, Ahidjo had Ernest Ouandie, Gabriel Tabeu, and Raphael Fotsing shot on Bamileke soil in the town of Bafoussam, on January 15, 1971, as a way of teaching the brave and hardworking Bamileke people of Cameroon another lesson in political intolerance on his part. Bishop Ndongmo simply vanished into thin air to most of us, until long after when word seeped out that the Reverend man was with his pastoral father in Rome—the Supreme Pontiff, Pope Paul VI. All we had heard on the grapevine was that as determined as Ahidjo was to kill Bishop Ndongmo, in spite of his pronouncements to the contrary, he could not afford to bring the wrath of the Vatican onto his regime. According to the rumours circulating, Cameroon's most trusted method of disseminating even government policies most of the time, Pope Paul VI had given Ahidjo an ultimatum that was not less than a diplomatic threat: "Ahidjo can kill Ndongmo, but I want my Bishop." It is a stupid cockroach that would attempt to wrestle with a chicken. Ahidjo had more sense, and so according to rumours again, he let Ndongmo leave Cameroon for the Vatican ultimately, where he lived until he died naturally in 1992. The truth, however, is that the late Bishop did not go to the Vatican but to Canada where he lived as a Canadian citizen until his death. The Bishop was buried in the premises of his cathedral in Bafoussam. How else could a nation be best divided against itself? The Bamilekes have not forgotten the massacre of their people, and although they remain a quiet and hardworking people, a rape victim does not forget her ordeal even if she will not talk about it. The Bamilekes died in large numbers as Ahidjo paved his way into power and subsequently dictatorship. Backed by French forces, for example, soldiers from La République stormed Tombel on several occasions and killed large numbers of Bamileke, men, women, and children who had escaped from La République and settled in Tombel.

With his Francophone political rivals and enemies neutralized, Ahidjo could now give West Cameroon his undivided attention. He announced that in a referendum Cameroonians had decided to become one people by eliminating the divisive and equally expensive federal system for a unitary system of government. Once more, the nomads were on the move: the country's name became The United Republic of Cameroon, ditching the Federal Republic of Cameroon. While West Cameroonians, like true nomads at a new site, were still having teething problems contemplating and getting used to the country's new name, Ahidjo went to work immortalizing West Cameroon's second-class status and dependency on East Cameroon. He disbanded, banned, and somehow manoeuvred West Cameroon political parties into oblivion; the House of Chiefs suffered a similar fate. Then like a joke, one started hearing French programs over Radio Buea, programs designed to teach West Cameroonians French; hence the program "French by Radio." Even then, our parents were expected to attend French lesson classes after returning home from work by 3:30pm as was the case in those days before the current and equally obnoxious two-shift system which deprives families of any quality time. The Roman Catholic Mission School Buea Town, served as the center where my father was expected to attend French classes. Our parents laughed at the idea of them returning to school; little did they know they were tentative pioneers of an embarrassing if not shameful identity being accorded their progeny. They were the seeds that were to yield partial alienation and total chaos to a once established people—Southern Cameroonians. In the same vein, French was also introduced in West Cameroon schools and in due course made a compulsory subject. In other words, a student had to earn a pass grade in this foreign tongue in order to move on to the next grade. This was quite an effective strategy at ensuring this bitter pill was swallowed, thus guaranteeing a future generation of West Cameroonians with the East Cameroonian's linguistic competence and culture at the very least. In this way, the plan of subjugation gathered momentum.

Ahidjo could no longer wait for our parents to master the French language. As soon as he was convinced they had the basics, he moved them into French speaking territories of Cameroon where they had no choice but to master the language while on the job. It worked: West Cameroonians quickly learned French to perfection to survive in East Cameroon, but they never forgot their original identity.

On the other hand, Ahidjo sent Francophones over into West Cameroon and gave them positions of authority. Accordingly, they could not care less about English as, from a position of power, they administered in the heart of West Cameroon in French. The picture was becoming clear: the government intended Cameroon's bilingualism for West Cameroonians not East Cameroonians. Before long, these French-speaking (Francophone) administrators displayed a level of corruption never before seen in West Cameroon; not even their being exposed led to any punitive consequences as would have been the case during the West Cameroon days. Their promotions, in fact, kept coming as if by mismanaging West Cameroon's institutions, administrative and financial alike, they were following their job descriptions closely. Of course, it was not long before the once established administrative and financial bastions of West Cameroon started collapsing: the Bota Oil Mill was closed; most of the offices in Buea were closed and the documents carted away and dumped along corridors in Yaounde; the wharf in Bota was closed, leading to the asphyxiation of all the super stores in West Cameroon; the Yoke dam which supplied low-cost electricity to West Cameroonians was also closed down for no obvious reasons. Slowly but surely, West Cameroon was losing her autonomy as she became heavily dependent on East Cameroon for capital, especially with the introduction of the French franc into West Cameroon where a version of the Pound Sterling was being used. Then Ahidjo disbanded the dreaded West Cameroon Police Mobile Wing unit, renowned for its discipline. After Ahidjo witnessed these men on parade in Buea in the late sixties, their discipline and mastery of military tactics scared him, and because they had no parallel in East Cameroon, they had to go. The police force itself was then deformed. Their uniforms changed from the well-ironed pair of shorts, which was once khaki, then it was changed to a navy-blue terylene material, softer to the touch, and finally to one that reminded my childhood mind of a woman's outfit with pockets around the thighs. Even their ranks changed and had no meaning to the West Cameroonian, with police officers themselves struggling to identify the ranks, which had now lost all the power that used to be associated with them.

From the days of the lance corporal, corporal, sergeant, inspector, the superintendent of Police, the senior superintendent of Police, to the Commissioner of Police, we now heard of *Gardien de la Paix*, *Gardien de la Paix Principale*. For a brief while there was the Brigadier rank in the police force, but it disappeared by the late seventies or early eighties, then there was the *Inspecteur*, *Inspecteur de Police Principale*, *Officier*, *Officier de Police Principale*, then *Commissaire*, *Commissaire de Police Principale*, and lastly *Divisionaire*. From *Officier de Police* they carried a golden star until they had six golden stars at the rank of the *Divisionaire*. The only rank that made some sense to most of us from West Cameroon was the "Inspecteur;" it sounded like the inspector we knew, and were aware of the fact that these were superior and equally powerful police officers. An inspector in the West Cameroon Police Force was a top ranking officer with about fifty other police officers under his command. Accordingly, like the rest of the police force, they were extremely disciplined and rarely encountered in uniform outside of their offices. These new *Inspecteurs de Police* were mostly undisciplined drunks who were always out on traffic control, unlike the West Cameroon Police Force that had special traffic officers way below the rank of an inspector. The new force was made up of men and women who were masters and mistresses of nothing else other than collecting bribes and harassing civilians whom they should be protecting. To this new police force, the uniform did not inspire discipline as it did the men and women of the West Cameroon Police force; it was instead a mark of authority and power, which they could use at will to abuse the unfortunate citizen and taxpayer who had nobody to whom they could bring up a complaint.

7

It was sometime in 1968 that West Cameroonians learned with certainty that the new police force, unlike the old, was trained to be the enemy instead of the friend of the citizenry. It must have been 4:00am, very early in the morning one day with families still soundly asleep when we heard heavy insane banging on our main door. My father was at the door in no time only to find that the hoodlums were in fact uniformed police officers. They were asking for all kinds of nonsense—identification papers, receipts for electronic gadgets, even those as old as, if not older than some of the officers were and so on. My father identified himself as a police officer before stepping out into the morning hours to look for and protest to the officer in charge. This must have been my very first encounter with the French language besides the gibberish a few friends already in French speaking schools used to babble on the playground. My childhood neighbor, a certain Henry, was attending a French speaking school and he used to sing some strange songs to us that made it even harder for us to tell what French words could be like. On this dreadful morning when order died in West Cameroon, all the officers were shouting at us in French even as my father spoke back in English, only for them to demonstrate that he was not making sense to them. His identity card was all that made some sense to them, especially as the uniform he had on was that of the original West Cameroon Police Force. Frustrated by the lack of communication between him and his colleagues supposedly, my father stormed off after instructing us to stay within and not open the door for anyone.

Having waited for my father to return to the bedroom in vain, my mother came out to the sitting room where we were. I told her what had transpired, and that my father was outside. Just then, another round of banging started. It was as if they were going to smash in the door if nobody answered. When my mother opened the door, she was only trying to locate my father in the darkness outside, and so did not even listen to the police man shouting angrily in French at her; not that she would have understood him either. As my mother moved to the side to avoid any contact with the intruding officer as she tried stepping out onto the veranda, he struck her with a stick in her thigh. It must have stung my mother as she immediately turned clawing and shouting at the police officer who had struck an unarmed woman. I launched at the man below the waist level, given my height, punching and like an offended puppy, baring my teeth in readiness to bite, when our neighbour, Mr. Tanyi and his wife, tore mother and son off the cursing police man just as other police men rushed to the scene of the fracas. A lot of shouting ensued between the Tanyis and the uniformed men, each shouting in his own language. I remember Mr. Tanyi asking angrily if they were trained to go about beating up women and people's wives. He called them a thieving police force for going around at night instead of by day if indeed their job was for the good of the people. About an hour had gone by before my father returned to see my mother's swollen thigh. Fuming with anger and his nostrils flaring as he breathed, my father was determined to find the police man responsible for assaulting my mother, the police man who had struck his wife. This time out I accompanied him as he walked out again to look for the officer in charge to whom he had protested earlier on before returning home.

Even as a child, I could recognize the commanding officer. It was Mr. Chiabi, the fair-skinned police superintendent whom we, as kids, described as "pussy-eye" because his pupils were not exactly black but were like those of a cat instead. They must have put Mr. Chiabi in charge hoping he would be able to discipline the bunch of ragtag men under his command. Chiabi was Anglophone and possibly Ikeja if not Scotland Yard trained, but he was expected to control a bunch of men to whom discipline as members of a special corps—the police force—had no meaning. After protesting to Mr. Chiabi, my father and I waited until the men regrouped as ordered and were walking past in a single file and I identified the offender. I never knew what disciplinary sanctions might have been taken against him. However, seeing what the force is like today after years of associating with it, I am sure that, even if Mr. Chiabi reported this scoundrel to the disciplinary unit, that is if they had any at all, they did nothing to him. From the nonsense we see today, he might have been promoted instead for displaying enthusiasm at work. Whatever the case, one thing was becoming clearer to West Cameroonians—this was not the police force, as they had known it during the Southern Cameroons and West Cameroon days. These were uniformed thugs good at nothing else other than brutalizing unarmed civilians, something that would have earned them a severe sanction in the days of the West Cameroon Police Force.

Like a cancer at work, the ways of West Cameroon were slowly and in most cases obtrusively invaded, contaminated, and almost totally obliterated by the ways of East Cameroon, because of our coming together within the United Republic of Cameroon. I do not say this to disrespect the East Cameroonian, but to point out the plain truth. Their ways of doing things, comparatively speaking, lacked the strict discipline that was in West Cameroon. They just did not seem to care about the nation but about their private needs, as opposed to the concern for the state and nationhood that reigned in West Cameroon. Consequently, to attempt denying that the colonial cultures we inherited are vastly different is to be dishonest to oneself. At the very least, it is the clash and subsequent fusion of the colonial culture with the indigenous and the attendant concoction that emerged. It is the same thing happening to Francophone education today as we see many Francophones switching to Anglophone schools because of the nature of our curricula. In spite of this, Francophone leaders are either too foolishly conceited, ignorant, or plainly in denial to acknowledge that there has to be something better in the Anglophone educational set-up for the nation to investigate and if need be adopt this system of education for the entire nation. To do that would amount to conceding to Anglophone values and this to the Francophone majority government is ridiculous. West Cameroonians, in like manner, saw their sanitation officers who were called "Sanintri," a corruption of "Sanitary," die out until we got to a point where it is now all right to dump dirt in the streets without being arrested for littering and worst of all without feeling any sense of guilt for such irresponsible behaviour. This is certainly alien to West Cameroon. Again, we saw men and women in uniform degenerating into government owned and sponsored bandits. In West Cameroon, there was zero tolerance for officers of the law who got involved in crime; they were dismissed, tried, and sentenced accordingly. In East Cameroon, on the other hand, the officers instead used their uniforms as empowering agents to facilitate the committing of crimes. There was now no longer any respect for government property as those in power wasted government resources while stealing from the government. Those with state vehicles, for example, turned them into their private property, using them for private family business after working hours, to the point of blatantly parking these vehicles in their private premises over the night. There was now absolutely no accountability; order was freefalling into chaos. Today we are at a point where even human life no longer means anything. Criminals slaughter innocent citizens on a daily basis without the police making any arrests ever, nor does the government render any apologies to the public, in spite of the thousands of police officers milling the streets idly yet on very high salaries paid by the taxpayer.

Chaos is now the way of life, with a president who cares less about Cameroonians, even if Cameroon were only his private estate, as it seems, given the arbitrary and nonchalant manner in which he is administering the country. People take better care of their lawns than Biya does of Cameroon. It is not surprising it was said Ahidjo handed over Cameroon to Biya because he knew Biya would destroy the country and so he, Ahidjo, would appear indispensable. The result is that West Cameroonians have died in their numbers deeply troubled about the nature of the union into which they have led their progeny. The government takes decisions without consulting with the people, nor does the government have any plans for the future. The issue now is who has enough contacts or is well placed himself to begin stealing from the government for himself. Look at people celebrating after being appointed to government positions because of the opportunity to pilfer having been granted them. Men without a single car are appointed ministers of state and within a year have many cars lining their premises.

Bribery is now the norm, so much so that Cameroonians under the age of thirty have never experienced a time in their nation's history when deserved services were rendered without bribery and corruption. Cameroon today is a mess, so much so that one has, virtually, to bribe even in a bank to deposit one's money into one's account; it is that bad. Not only are most workers unqualified mindful of the fact that they got their jobs through corrupt means rather than by merit, they just do not care. A manager with a sense of purpose, for example, is helpless since trying to discipline an indolent, corrupt, irresponsible worker may mean stepping on the toes of the president's wife or some equally powerful member of the clique of thieves misdirecting the nation, and this would certainly lead to the loss of his job. The outcome then, is a certain nonchalance and helplessness appropriately summed up in a pidgin expression "how man go do?"

The Unfortunate thing about the status quo is that West Cameroonians who knew better have become so adept at copying instead of standing up against these malpractices. After my high school, my father pointed out that I was not to go to the university in Cameroon because of the chaos he heard reigned there along with professors' tendency to want to hold students back for ridiculous reasons. At the time, we had just one miserable university, which even one of Cameroon's leading scholars Bernard Fonlon had described as a glorified high school. My father, who is now late, never could understand why someone in a university, studying subjects he or she likes should fail at the rate our children were failing in Yaounde. He had a friend he was very proud of who used to teach at the university whom he blamed all the time as if the poor man alone were responsible for the problems in Yaounde. "What is it with all these re-writing of exams?" my father would query in disgust. "You who studied in the white man's land, is this how their own children keep re-writing exams and failing? Because to me that simply means something is wrong with the teachers, right?" I watched them with keen interest during such conversations, but all his friend did was smile quietly without ever giving a befitting answer in response. Accordingly, I was encouraged to teach with my advanced level certificate before going on. A group of ex-students was on the staff list at Sacred Heart College at the time: Godwin Sendze, Jean Tanda, the late Jaff Kweban aka Chookash, Vincent Che, and Samuel Takwi. We went on teaching until sometime in 1980 when Paul Kwenkam aka Paulus returned on a visiting trip during one holiday period and encouraged all of us to join him at the University of Ibadan. He confirmed that the standards were incredibly high, and a student passed if he or she merited it. The following year, through the Joint Admissions and Matriculations Board, we all registered at Ibadan in different departments though and so did our university years begin in an institution where we met with excellent standards. Our professors were the best in their field and were as confident as any true authority could be. Here I was set on fire by scholars like Professors Dan Izevbaye, Niyi Osundare, Isidore Okpewho, Joseph Egberike, Albert Olu Ashaolu, and

Chikwneye Okonjo Ogunyemi to name a few. Students who asked questions did not intimidate them as we had heard was the case in Yaounde, and so this was just great. In fact, one had to challenge Professor Niyi Osundare if one were to score well in his class. Professor Dan Izevbaye would smile gently as he listens to a student challenging him. He encouraged you and then doused your stance with great ideological propositions and trends that left one wondering how much time these men of letters spent reading if not studying. It was normal to run into Professor Okpewho in the research section of the library working like any other graduate student. In this way, they instilled in us the will to carry out serious, worthwhile research; and so the years came and went, and in spite of some challenges like the university closing down because of students going on strike, one was ultimately blessed to earn a distinguished and equally internationally respected terminal degree. My dream then was to return home and contribute in my own way to the development of young minds in my native country, but first, I had to get a job with the university in Cameroon and this was one hell of an experience.

I had to navigate very dangerous waters with other colleagues determined to get their friends or relatives hired instead of the Ph.D. and best qualified candidate for the position. They demanded all kinds of documents from me; even my defense report was required. I could not help questioning what university required a defense report for recruiting faculty if this is not just to make it impossible for the candidate's file to be complete. The defense report is the property of the university where the defense took place and so only a corrupt system like Yaounde's at the time, could be asking for a document they knew the candidate could not possess. Even after that, a member of the search committee deliberately left one of my documents in his office on the day the applicants' files were being studied by the search committee so as to complain that my file was not complete. Of course, this would have meant the disqualification of my application, but my documents had been submitted by another colleague who knew the system very well, and so he had ensured that the receiving colleague tick on a duplicate list all the documents that were in my file that had been submitted to him. Consequently, when at the very last minute this very influential but corrupt member of the search committee rejected my application on the basis that my file was incomplete, the bearer of my documents reminded him that he was the one who submitted it and that he had indicated on his own list that my file was complete. In this manner, this frustrated and equally unethical scholar was forced to "suspect" that he must have left the document on his table. He retrieved the document and my recruitment went through. Of course, he had not forgotten my document; he had deliberately left it behind, hoping that the position would be given to a doctorat de 3me cycle candidate of his on the basis that my dossier was incomplete, thanks to his ingenuity. Even from Nigeria, another African country, I was already used to things moving smoothly, so one could imagine my frustration at the system I ran into in Cameroon. I was shocked that even some scholars who had studied in North America had returned to Cameroon and were worse at virtually everything they did when pitted against those who had never left the country. They were vicious to students and colleagues alike and stood in the path of their progress, a bane they never experienced in North America. Some hoarded information that could lead to professional growth on the part of faculty and benefitted from it alone. For example, because of the chaos within the university system that treats its different colleges and schools as if they are rivals instead of different arms of the university system, information that could benefit faculty as a whole, such as international grants and fellowships, never got to the university colleges and schools in the provinces. Even colleagues one expected would have been open minded enough never shared such information with others in the provinces until they had benefitted from it themselves. Yet how myopic such a disposition could be, especially from scholars, for it is a basic saying that what goes around comes around. The people of Mankon say, "If you do something good to somebody, you will also reap something good in return else your child is somewhere benefitting as a result of your good deed." By being of help to somebody today, one may not realize that one is only helping oneself. How often has a former student or an unknown person rescued one from a tight situation? The helping hand then narrates the help one was to him sometime back, which one might have forgotten even, yet some of our scholars continue to treat our young ones in school and even their colleagues like dirt. I will never forget the warning issued me by a dear friend when I was recruited into the university in Cameroon. He called the name of another Cameroonian colleague of Anglophone origin and warned me sternly "No matter what, do not let your paths cross. This guy is vicious." I made sure my path and the culprit's never crossed, yet I saw how he victimized and destroyed others and I could not be more grateful to my friend. I went on with my job as a university professor, enjoying every moment of it. I was already married, with kids, and but for the Anglophone albatross about my neck, life was great. This is where I was in life when the landmark presidential elections of 1992 were held.

8

Over half a century has gone by, and as we look back at Southern Cameroons, one thing is so stark about this so-called "reunion with our brothers and sisters across the Mungo": it has been a most expensive reunification for the Southern Cameroonians. We have, in the process, lost almost everything we had before joining East Cameroon, yet the abusive and equally exploitative trend is still forging on like ever. In many ways, the Francophone dominated government makes Anglophones to feel that we do not belong, we are not native to the Republic of Cameroon, and indeed, we are not. The government treats us as national bastards, the side effects of cold war politics, refugees of history fashioned by the vicious diplomatic trend of a now irrelevant era, destined never to belong, at best nominal nomads to be called this today and that tomorrow. Hence, in his anger and frustration, the late Anglophone scholar, Bate Bessong, declared us "beasts of no nation." We rejected Nigeria of our own freewill to join citizens of La République du Cameroun, with whom we once belonged, even under the Germans, before being partitioned and served as compensation to France and Britain, only to find out belatedly that the cultural punch of British and French ways had transformed, if not deformed, each group beyond recognition. The truth is there are some amongst us who, with good reasons, think enough is enough, and so we should go our separate ways. Yet there are others who think we have put in too much just to turn around and walk away like that—our labour forces have been exploited, our resources drained, and our institutions obliterated or fractured at the very least. This latter group thinks we ought to stay and fight for recognition and equality. Yet how does one reason with a people whose heads are buried in sand pits? How does one reason with a people who refuse to be honest, even with themselves, the basic spice for any relationship or social interaction. Have we not tried dialoguing only for Mr. Paul Biya and his cohorts to declare a national conference "sans objet"? Yet in a most unashamedly arrogant manner, he and an accursed few squander our national resources as if they are privately owned, while the rest of the population is willing to sit quietly, afraid to speak up. In the process, shockingly, some continue celebrating along tribal lines who is in office and who is not, as if a tribesman being appointed minister or prime minister immediately guarantees welfare for individuals of the said ethnic group or the ethnic group as a whole even.

The French-speaking majority has attacked everything West Cameroon in this union, contaminating what they cannot eradicate or destroy at once. If not for the fact that for once, Southern Cameroonians remembered their history and stood up as one voice against destructive changes, what would have happened to our most effective system of education? They would have abolished it for some démodé Napoleonic curriculum. Yet, here are students from La République du Cameroun abandoning the old Napoleonic curriculum their leaders are clinging to, which even the "motherland" had rejected, to benefit from a tried Southern Cameroons' system of education.

Whenever the opportunity presents itself, the Cameroun nation uses her troops to attack, torture, and kill Southern

Cameroonians without any qualms. When Southern Cameroonians protest, they are branded insulting names like "Biafrans" or "the enemies in the house," yet they refuse to sit like civilized people to listen to our complaints. Denying addressing the truth does not make it go away; the onus is only postponed with this display of irresponsibility. How can we forget then that we do not belong in a nation where one sleeps with one's eyes open, a nation where leaders are thieves, a nation that unleashes armed rag tag soldiers to kill their own citizens because they are Southern Cameroonians and so are expendable? Has everything not been done to destroy Southern Cameroon? The latest trick being to separate us into two different units, and now they continue to remind one unit—the South West—of its closer cultural similarities with the Douala's instead of their historical belonging with the Grassfielders? If the Bakweris will permit such an amorphous argument to persuade them and pit them against the other Southern Cameroons' unit, then the people of Mamfe should begin celebrating their nearness and even go on rampage in an effort to reunite with a better thriving Calabar people and culture in neighbouring Nigeria, because their culture is virtually the same. To say the least, the culture of the people of Mamfe is just as identical, if not more, with that of the people of Calabar than is the Bakweri culture to Douala's, but this is never mentioned nor is it important, since the goal is to divide and rule Southern Cameroonians within Cameroun, and some of our leaders fall into this trap. And so ridiculously, the South West celebrates victory when the post of Prime Minister is taken from a Bamenda man and given to a South Westerner, and vice versa. How one mourns for those brave Southern Cameroonians of yesterday—Dr. E.

M. L. Endeley, Bobe Ngom Jua, John Ngu Foncha—and the rest, even the Elads and Anyangwes of more recent years who put Southern Cameroons first before their ethnic groups, their stomachs, and personal bank accounts. Alas this is an era when just anyone can jump up and talk, hence the confusion and occasional animosity reigning within the West Cameroon camp as some of our own, some hiding behind grey beards, sow seeds of discord for a little purse instead of struggling to build a better nation for our children whom we see drowning into servitude and oblivion should the trend continue unchecked.

See what they did to their own people in Douala and Bafoussam who followed Bamenda and Kumba's cue at protesting against the stolen presidential election results of 1992. John Fru Ndi had emerged with the qualities of a true messiah—a humble, hardworking background and speaking up against a corrupt government on behalf of the suffering lot of the masses—and so we all fell in behind this brave son hoping to oust a comatose regime that had degenerated into a liability to the proletariat. Workers' retirement investments had been mismanaged and stolen leaving honest, retired civil servants without pensions for which they contributed. Salaries had been reduced by about 70% taking the devaluation of the franc into consideration; banks, like other businesses, were closing down leaving citizens unemployed and some without their deposits into such banks. Meanwhile, Cameroon's resources and national investments were being sold or mortgaged to foreigners. As a nation, Cameroon was as good as dead even as Biya continued insulting the citizens and bragging about the number of years he had left in the presidency. How I wish he had simply declared he would live forever. In the face of such disastrous leadership and insults, it is not surprising then that with one voice, the people of Cameroon wanted him out in 1992; a position indicative of the possibility of a true Anglophone-Francophone union but for the misleading role played by selfish political leaders with regards to the Anglophone predicament. Even his own native province at the time and his personal staff at the presidency voted Biya out. But like most idiotic African leaders, this personification of failure wanted power at all cost, causing the nation to erupt after he, instead of John Fru Ndi, was declared winner of the 1992 presidential elections.

I was in the Catholic Church in Bali, a participant in the Requiem Mass for my dear friend and school mate, the late Engineer Charles Fofang, who had died a day or two before, when the allegedly cooked up election results were announced proclaiming Biya the winner. A strange silence hung in the air; I was later to find out that it was caused by the shock and disbelief generated by this national lie. We filed out to the cemetery and buried Charlie Boy, as his close friends called him, and then, sensing that all was not going to be alright, those of us from Mankon and its environs immediately embarked on the roughly twelve-fifteen kilometres drive back to Mankon town. It was around Mile 90 on the way to Mankon that I realized our hunches were being transformed into reality. Groups of people, mostly young men and women were streaming to town as if there was an agreed meeting and a venue.

At the entrance into Mankon, just before the National Cooperative College, I met the first barricade and a mad crowd; they recognized my car.

"Doctor, where are you from on a day like this?" Someone questioned. It was rhetorical; however, I answered hoping the word "death" would soften them.

"I am from burying my friend in "Bali,"" I answered back doing all to look as sad as I could.

"Sorry Doctor, but things are bad, eh, Doc. Just look for a place and park your car because you cannot get into town." I found out later on that they were right. They were the first mad crowd erecting a huge barricade in protest against the rigged election results. It was their hope that by blockading the city and making it hard for people to move, the police would be called in and it would lead to a confrontation that would draw the government's attention to the fact that people did not buy their lie. There was another barricade just after the entrance into the National Cooperative College, one further into town about a mile in front of a wine and beer Off-license popularly referred to as "Travellers'"; there was another about half a mile further into town around Presbyterian Church, Azire, and so on. So between where I was and my parents' compound, under half a mile towards the heart of Mankon town, there were two barricades with tyres already burning in the centre of these barricades. There was no way I could get my car into my father's compound where it would be reasonably safe. Even then, how would my wife and I have made our house all the way across town? The thought of driving through town to my own house at Ngomgham was completely out. I could imagine at least eight such barricades along this route before my house. I had to drive past Ntarinkon, John Fru Ndi's neighbourhood, which turned out to be the main stage for the unfolding drama. But Mankon is my town, and I had a good knowledge of virtually every motorable stretch. So I made up my mind to use back routes to get to my house, hoping the major roads were the ones being barricaded. Even then, I had to get past this first barricade which was about forty feet before the road branches off to the left into Ntaturu. My plan was to go through Ntaturu, dart across the Mankon-Mbengwi main road into Alakuma, then emerge on the Mankon-Bafut road, turn right and go for about two hundred meters and then turn left onto the Bamenda Urban Council Road, which also leads to Ngomgham, and I would be home.

I did not plead for long before the angry young men decided to make a small opening to the side of the barricade for me to sneak through.

"Hey open that end a little, let Doctor go through there."

"Thanks! Thanks!" I quipped to the young man who had suddenly confirmed himself the leader of the bunch.

"Doctor, just use the back roads and go home if you can. Things are bad."

"Thanks," I called out as I went through the barricade. As I turned left towards Ntaturu, I heaved a sigh of relief, but my heart was already racing. My wife sitting by me was dead quiet as she took in everything without a word, possibly wondering how things could degenerate into such lawlessness so suddenly.

I made it through Ntaturu, across the Mankon-Mbengwi road into Alakuma, and was beginning to relax, feeling good about what a wonderful thing it is for me to know my way around town, when I saw the smoke in the air in the distance. It was as if my heart stopped beating at that tell-tale sign, then the barricade itself came into view. Thank God! The barricade was still being erected about a hundred meters from the Mankon-Bafut road. I was well known in this neighbourhood. I greeted the crowd and edged my way across the barricade, swung right on the Mankon-Bafut road, sped up a little slope and was about to turn left towards Ngomgham when I met my ultimate test. Once more, there was angry shouting and the dishing of orders to nobody in particular. This was my neighbourhood. I drove past this spot every day, sometimes as many as ten times a day even. It was my main route into town and so I knew virtually everybody around here and vice versa. Unlike in the other neighbourhoods where I was begging, in an authoritative manner I asked the boys to open up and they immediately did. "I will be back," I called out as I zoomed away leaving a trail of dust in the air. At last I drove in through the gate into my fenced-in compound and felt safe as my German shepherd came charging: its way of saying welcome. I got in, changed into a more casual and equally comfortable outfit and a pair of canvas shoes. With a torchlight in my hand, since it was already dark, I started walking back towards the last barricade I had encountered on my way home. "Be careful!" my wife called out as I disappeared into the surrounding darkness.

As I walked on, I thought of all I had been through that day; I knew it was going to be a long night as I heard the urban area humming and buzzing with activity. Virtually everyone not at a barricade was marching towards Fru Ndi's Ntarinkon residence, with some brandishing torchlights and others lighted lanterns. Slowly, and with an ominous air hovering over Bamenda, time passed. It was 1:00 a.m. when I picked my way back home completely exhausted even as my heart turned to my deceased friend spending his first night in the belly of the earth. I thought of our times together, his laughter, his dreams, and the occasional bottle of Beaufort before him and a half-empty glass in his grip.

"Doc, you are already coming back?"

"Yes!" I answered unable to recognize the speaker.

"Okay, we are on our way then. See you tomorrow."

"Be careful!" I called out. "I am sure those uniformed people will soon be out and about."

One could hear our strides headed in opposite directions as our silhouettes disappeared in the darkness. Once in a while, I would flick on and off my torchlight to confirm an undulation in the dirt road; otherwise, I walked on in the darkness wondering what was in store come the next day.

The very next day the town was dead quiet; not a soul seemed to stir, not even the birds. The atmosphere stood still but portentous. I ventured out of my fenced-in compound and saw a few dressed-up people who seemed to be on their way to work, and then a lone private car would amble past on its way. Words trickled into the neighbourhood that there was a heavy police presence along the main streets, and they were going around clearing the streets of barricades as people looked on from their yards or from the security of their homes. The majority stayed home rather dare an encounter with angry uniformed men in an effort to go to work. The day went by fast, and by evening there were all kinds of rumours about intentions to arrest the main opposition leader—John Fru Ndi—from his Ntarinkon residence where he was already hemmed in, under house arrest, with scores of his party's members and supporters. The result was that before 6:00 p.m., thousands of men and women, the young and the old, had surrounded the compound, trapping in even the gendarme officers who had barricaded the way into Fru Ndi's compound, as a way of protecting Fru Ndi. One could hear the town buzzing. Even then, the night went by, extraordinarily quiet; sounds could be heard from far away that would not have been possible otherwise. The sound of a shot would crack out in the seemingly serene nocturnal air echoing from horizon to horizon; a lone dog would howl, bark suddenly and briefly as if unsure of what it was barking at, then all would become dead quiet again.

By Wednesday morning the people of Bamenda, already armed with a better understanding of the government's decision to flood Bamenda with soldiers who must do all to maintain peace, stood up to a new, boisterous but unpredictable day. Many were convinced the day would not come to a peaceful end even as they, with private vehicles parked safely at home and taxis not working, were already trekking to work. The surviving barricades, since the small number of police men and women could not clear everything, made it impossible for taxis to do good business, and some of the drivers kept away as a way of protesting their stolen presidential election victory. Some private cars, mainly, could be seen meandering in and out of back streets as the owners did all they could to get to work. Those without cars had to trek miles to work with the sun and the heat. I used to wonder how they felt when they got to work—sweaty and sticky. It is not surprising then that the prices for colognes and deodorants shot up in stores. The most surprising thing of all was the way some car owners treated some pedestrians, even those they knew. Whereas many car owners gave rides joyfully to workers they met on their way to work, ending up with crowded cars, there were others who drove to work ignoring the pedestrians they saw on the way. One case I found particularly interesting was that of this woman who lived by the comatose Bamenda airport whose husband was supposed to be a researcher, or was she the researcher herself, I do not know. I once saw her drive past another lady she knew very well, without as much as casting a glance in her direction. Because I was just a few steps behind the lady on foot, I asked her if that was not the woman I saw since I knew them to be friends or at the very least acquaintances. The gentle lady who was trekking simply smiled and said nothing. Usually very well dressed and beautiful, her young family was yet to buy a car, and so her friend had, thanks to the uprising, found an area in which she believed she was above the lady walking to work. The advantage was short-lived, as the husband of the lady on foot drove into Bamenda a new car for his family within a week as if reacting to the "insult" given his wife by a friend. It was interesting, almost as if nature was trying to warn the lady on foot about her so-called friend.

By late afternoon this Tuesday, armed gendarmes and policemen in uniform were carried about town in trucks in a show of force; they stopped and removed the surviving barricades in their way and continued driving on. They believed the barricades were responsible for vehicles—taxis included—not being driven about. Interestingly, as the uniformed men pushed the barricades off the streets and drove on, as soon as they were out of sight, groups of young men suddenly emerged from their homes and reinstalled the barricades. Some were made up of huge trees that had just been felled so they fell on to the road blocking traffic. There were the carcasses of old vehicles, huge trucks, and even bulldozers used as barricades. I was never able to figure out how these carcasses were manoeuvred into place. At the bridge between City Chemist Round-about and Sonac Street, these carcasses were not only put in place but were welded to the bridge even as flames and smoke rose into the air from the tyres burning deep within the core of these barricades. Bamenda, like a dormant volcano, had erupted. By night, thousands of men, women, and even teenagers wound their way to John Fru Ndi's compound to protect him and only walked back to their homes after dawn even as a fresh crowd installed itself in place. Once it was rumoured that Fochivé, the notorious head of Paul Biya's Gestapo, was, in the form of a snake, going to get to Fru Ndi; any snake caught around Fru Ndi's compound following the rumour was not only killed but battered to death, hacked into pieces, and then doused with fuel and burned. A dog shared the same fate when the rumours claimed a dog was Fochivé's latest form in his effort to reach Fru Ndi.

There were many clashes between civilians and government troops as the latter struggled, in vain, to eliminate the barricades. The result, typical of La République's armed forces, was the use of force. Truckloads of soldiers went around arresting young men whom they ran into on the streets without any provocation whatsoever. This was the situation in Bamenda when one day news got down to the people that not only was there going to be reinforcements sent into Bamenda to help the already exhausted armed forces and police, but that there were orders for the arrest of Fru Ndi and other top ranking officials of the main and, as of then, only reliable political party, The Social Democratic Front (SDF). That was all the provocation

Bamenda needed. That evening, the people went to work. They dug trenches about four feet deep and four feet wide across major back roads leading into Bamenda town. Those roads that were tarred, and the people did not want to destroy, were covered with used engine oil which made them slippery. This was the case from the station end of Finance Junction going up Bamenda Station; the government residential area. Sections of the runway of the quiescent Bamenda airport were covered in engine oil so a plane could not land or take off in case the government thought of flying in reinforcements. With this done, the citizens were sure to see or hear should the authorities try to sneak in any reinforcements after dark by making them trek into Bamenda.

At the same time, secret police squads were raiding the homes of S.D.F. officials. Lawyer Sendze's home along Foncha's Street was ransacked by uniformed hoodlums supposed to be officers of the law, yet this was a distinguished attorney and citizen. Unable to locate husband and wife, the secret police unit destroyed property and valuables leaving a post hurricane scenario for the public to see. The distinguished lawyer, it was claimed, had fled to his village in Nso which even the most daring men in uniform could not dare approach under the existing atmosphere, let alone talk of locating him. True to the activities of such Gestapos, Lawyer Mrs. Sendze was later arrested and taken to the Brigade Mixte Mobile (BMM) where she was detained with other S.D.F. party barons like Lawyer Sama, and Alhadji Oumarou Sariki.

The tension downtown Bamenda was palpable. The population was determined nobody was to be carried out of Bamenda detention units to Yaounde. Their argument was simple: a government that had earned the people's vote of no confidence was framing responsible citizens by accusing them of crimes against the state. If this were true, then these accused persons would stand trial in Bamenda and nowhere else, after all Bamenda was a provincial capital like any other in Cameroon. How often are "criminals" accused of whatever crime in the French speaking parts of Cameroon, or East Cameroon, if you will, taken to Buea or Bamenda for trial? Why then were English speaking citizens to be transported from Bamenda, where they had been arbitrarily arrested and were yet to be charged of a crime, to a French speaking part of the country for their trial when they do not even understand French if the government intended to be transparent? Bamenda people knew if these sons and daughters of theirs were successfully taken across the Mungo, the river separating Anglophone from Francophone Cameroon, then they would be murdered. Accordingly, the people of Bamenda, with one voice, said "no" to the government's plan of transferring the detainees to Yaounde. There was nothing that showed or proved Yaounde or anywhere else a better place for these detainees.

The whole plan by the government reminded West Cameroonians in Bamenda that the forces of law and order of La République amounted to a force of occupation determined to teach the indigenes a lesson. Time was to prove them right. With Bel Luc-Réné aka Bend Look Grenade's Provincial Administration having informed Yaounde of Bamenda's decision accordingly, La République's government went to work and hatched what they were convinced was a plan that would be the final blow in subduing Bamenda and completely overriding West

Cameroon. It must be remembered that La République's government is to blame for West Cameroonians always seeing themselves as West Cameroonians instead of Cameroonians according to the scheme that yielded forth a United Republic. It is not surprising then that Paul Biya, mistaking the hour to be ripe, suddenly dismissed the "united" dimension to emerge with simply the Republic of Cameroon: Francophone Cameroun's name before they were reunited with Southern Cameroons. Hardly have a people been so burdened with sovereign nomenclatures and are yet to confirm any as befitting—from Southern Cameroonians under Britain, to West Cameroonians in the Federal Republic of Cameroon, to the United Republic of Cameroon, and today, to the Republic of Cameroon. Like nomads moving from place to place we keep moving from name to name, yet we are to be sure which is indeed ours as we continue to hear of Ambazonia on the side-lines.

9

It was September of 1992, when Paul Biya declared a State of Emergency in the North West Province of Cameroon after having been warned of the dimension things had taken in Bamenda. Initially, it meant little to the people until its implications started trickling down to the masses: there was going to be an all night curfew from 6:00 p.m. to 6:00 a.m. There would be no vehicles moving, everyone was to carry identification papers on his or her person and to make it immediately available to the forces of law[lessness] and [dis]order when demanded. The Mankon main market, which serves the Bamenda urban town, was to remain permanently closed, yet the people were expected to show up for work and on time. Slowly, it dawned on the population that Biya and his government were out not to make peace by addressing the issues that had enthroned disorder in the nation, but to prove to the population of Bamenda, especially, where power resided.

To effectively set the State of Emergency in place, heavily armed soldiers and police men and women from La République du Cameroun were dropped off at specific spots in particular neighbourhoods: Finance Junction, Mile 2 Nkwen, Mile 3 Nkwen, Mrs. Ngeng's Junction, Veterinary Junction, City Chemist Round About, Musang Junction, Hospital Round About, Atuakom Junction, Azire Old Church Junction, Traveller's Off-License, Bali Park area, Ntarinkon Market area especially, Bamenda Urban Council Junction, the entrance to Sacred Heart College, Ntsuabuh Junction, and so on. Bamenda, like a person's head with lice, was heavily infested with soldiers crawling around who enjoyed displaying how much leeway they had been authorized in their encounter and dealings with the supposedly rogue population. Biya was to learn first-hand what stuff the people of Bamenda are made of and what it meant to go against the population of Bamenda when they know they are right about something. It had been alleged that Ahmadou Ahidjo, upon relinquishing power warned Biya to be careful with Bamenda if he wanted a smooth ride, for which reason Biya quickly visited Bamenda after he took over. He must have forgotten the advice or else drunken by power he became reckless.

Slowly, but obviously, both camps, the heavily equipped but childishly excited soldiers on the one hand, and a population whose integrity and future were at stake on the other hand, sized each other up. The people kept their distance, doing all not to stand in groups as per the terms of the State of Emergency, yet the tension in the air was deep. Both camps knew it would take only some minor spark to ignite and set ablaze the smouldering inferno. Workers trekked to work and so did students and pupils to school, walking past arrogant yet suspicious soldiers in an atmosphere of silence that said a lot more than had it been otherwise. But then, strange circumstances are reputed for breeding strange bed mates.

Barely a few days had gone by when the government's own inadequacy and ineffectiveness started working against it. They had sown thousands of soldiers in the ideologically fertile fields of Bamenda, but had failed to consider the logistics for feeding these seeds. Soldiers went for days without food, and fasting not being a part of ordinary soldiers' routine, hunger humbled the once upon a time arrogant men and women in uniform. Before long, they went amidst their enemies, supposedly Bamenda people, begging for food. Hardly is there a province more accommodating than Bamenda. They fed the soldiers who, in due course, started realizing that Bamenda was not struggling for Bamenda alone, but for an oppressed, exploited, and abused nation. If listening to these theories and doctrines was all it took for the soldiers to eat, they emerged as a most devoted bunch of students. The result was friendship between the soldiers and their hosts who only a few days before had been presented to them as enemies of the state. The danger of this emerging fraternal relationship between the soldiers and the supposedly rogue province peaked when some soldiers had their guns "stolen" according to the government. What else could indicate how comfortable these soldiers had become in the midst of their enemies? The strategy of importing into Bamenda only French-speaking soldiers so as to maintain that gap between both camps had failed. The soldiers were getting the lessons of their lives in bourgeois and unpatriotic governance. The government's limping strategy to deal with their neglect of their soldiers was to shuffle the hungry soldiers about town. No soldier was to last more than several days at one spot.

This strategy might have worked had it been immediately employed from the onset; alas, it was a reaction to a problem which government helped create. By rotating already indoctrinated soldiers from one part of town to another every couple of days, the government unwittingly created the opportunity for the soldiers to compare notes and facts from one neighbourhood to the other. The government and soldiers alike were left wondering how a people could speak with one voice as such. Being humans, hostility soon turned into admiration for the people of Bamenda, but this transition spanned three months and, in between, a lot happened.

During the early days of their arrival, before hunger caused the soldiers and the government to reconsider their tactics, there were numerous clashes, sometimes bloody. Typical of La République's military, even after over a month later, the power drunk soldiers continued testing their prowess on innocent pedestrians and vandalizing homes on the whim. Woe betides, should a well-dressed young man happen on a handful of soldiers; they immediately went to work in an attempt to embarrass such a fellow. One example will better illustrate the mentality of these soldiers.

It was a Saturday evening and a young couple was walking back home, it seemed. They had just gone to one of those make-shift grocery markets that sprouted at sporadic road junctions to cater for the needs of the locals, since the main market was to remain closed until the gods in power felt Bamenda had been humbled enough. In these sporadic markets, virtually everything needed for preparing a meal was available. Market women, "buyam and sellam" as they are known locally, sold vegetables, fruits, and the rest, while men slaughtered and sold meat just nearby also. It was obvious from the contents of the baskets the young couple held, that they were from one such market in the neighbourhood when they happened upon a group of soldiers, about five in number, with automatic assault rifles dangling threateningly from their shoulders. As the couple moved from one side of the road to the other so as to avoid a head-on encounter with the soldiers, one of the soldiers ordered the couple to stop, which they did. Another soldier asked why they were on the streets in spite of the curfew.

"It is not yet 6:00 p.m." answered the young man.

"I did not ask you what time it is. I asked you why you are on the streets." It was a different soldier, short and stout in build.

"I understood you, which is why I told you it is not yet 6:00 p.m., unless you are telling me the curfew hours have changed."

"Okay," said the short stout soldier. "You think you are smart, right? Okay, put that basket down and drop on your knees. You!" directed at the young lady who was with the young man, "stand over there." The soldiers made the young man lie down in the mud even as numerous young men idling around looked on. They remembered they were not to sit in groups. One would have thought they cared less about what was going on until one of the soldiers literally stepped with his boots on the shin of the young man who had been rolling around in the mud with a stoical look on his face. Just then, all the young men from about a thirty meter circumference that, hitherto, had looked nonchalant, started walking towards the soldiers, the muddied young man, and the confused young woman who was already in tears. All of a sudden, the soldiers saw themselves surrounded by about fifty or sixty young men. From the group, a voice barked out at the young man: "Stand up." He hesitated as he scanned the faces of the soldiers.

"I said stand up!" came the voice again with a definite note of command. The young man stood up and looked at his dirty clothes whereas the soldiers just looked on perplexed as their predicament dawned on them. "Take the lady and go home," came another voice from within the group of young men that had just gathered. As the couple walked away, the soldiers looked on helplessly and with furtive glances from face to face in the crowd of young men who started trickling away after the couple was a safe distance away without any of the soldiers as much as uttering a word. Those in the outer layers of the crowd were already thawing away from the crowd of young men, when the roaring engine of a military personnel truck was heard in the distance. In a second, the crowd had disappeared leaving the hitherto perplexed handful of soldiers regaining their composure as once more they could breathe freely and look all around them, taking in the neighbourhood without being obstructed by layers of expressionless young faces that stared at them as if waiting for them to make one false move.

The arrival of the military truck was a huge relief; the soldiers who had been surrounded and had by now almost completely regained their wits, beckoned the driver to stop. Suddenly hit by the full impact of the near death experience they had just been through, they felt their legs buckling under them. Had the truck delayed by just a minute, the hitherto trapped soldiers, it seemed, would have needed help climbing into the truck behind which other soldiers who had already been picked up were chitchatting with obvious sighs of relief. The soldiers crashed onto the bare benches behind the truck as if they were sofas, unable to look elsewhere than at their own shoes as the truck roared and sputtered away into the distance. Whether or not these soldiers ever shared their ordeal with their friends will forever remain a mystery leaving one with options to conjecture: if they were a prideful bunch, then they swallowed their ordeal and only talked about it amongst themselves or else shared it and were ridiculed by the rest. Encounters like these were numerous.

On another occasion, during the State of Emergency, I had left my house in Ngomgham walking into town where my wife had been trapped behind enemy lines—the vandalizing troops of La République du Cameroun. As it happened from time to time during the State of Emergency, on this fateful day, a rather violent clash had erupted between civilians aka Force for Change on the one hand, and the Government troops on the other. One could hear from miles away the tear gas canisters being fired into the crowd, along with the whirring sound of a miserably lonely police chopper hovering in the skies over Bamenda like a sick and confused bird fallen behind in the wake of a migrating shoal. But this was Cameroon's police rehearsing war tactics against a civilian population it is supposed to be protecting, part of the tax paying force whose taxes pay their exaggerated salaries which transforms them into morons determined to kill civilians so as to maintain an unpopular autocrat in power.

"Bwap-bwap, bwap-bwap, bwap-bwap!" called the chopper's propellers as it carried both pilot and gunner hundreds of feet in the air, leaving tear gas canisters sailing down into the crowd, and at times life grenades we learned. The result is a number of daring young men without hands who, today, must beg to make a living. Who will accept that their enemies are members of their own nation's armed forces? This is the paradox of this marriage with La République. All too often I have caught myself wondering if these same soldiers who threw live grenades at the crowd in Bamenda would have done the same if they were facing a Yaounde or Mbalmayo crowd. At times these canisters blasted through the roofs of houses in residential areas, causing residents who had locked themselves indoors, hoping to remain safe within, diving out of their homes coughing and choking. In many cases, babies' lives were barely saved by an ever creative population that urged people to trace their nostrils with palm oil to keep off the tear gas, while others daubed their faces with towels or pieces of foam soaked in water. Then the rains, a very strange drizzle given the time of the year, came, and flooded homes with roofs destroyed by falling tear gas canisters. Nobody cared since it was the government blasting away at its own civilian population for protesting election results.

That my wife was in trouble was obvious, and it was my duty to rescue her or die trying. So I put on a pair of khaki trousers and a pair of Adidas Stan Smith canvas shoes I had, asked my house-help to stay indoors with the kids and not to answer the door until she heard me calling her name. I stepped out hoping to run into my wife on the way or make my way to her office by whatever means since that would mean having to face the soldiers at some point. I was also armed with my national identity and professional cards. The latter declares that I was a university professor and so, hopefully, would convince soldiers that I was a citizen of an exemplary nature and not likely to be one of those "vandals" attacking the government. What irony! That, of course, was dependent on the fact that I was asked to identify myself before I was gun-butted into pulp, and the latter was more likely: it was in searching the carcass of one more vandal that it would be discovered he was a university professor. This is how the troops of La République function. They beat the daylight out of you before asking you to identify yourself, only for them to realize you are not the person they were looking for and there is nothing that can be done. One can only imagine how the story would have been rephrased so as to praise a group of uniformed hoodlums for having killed a desperate husband and university professor out in a socio-political storm to save his trapped wife.

And so I stepped on the tarred road, which snakes its way from the Bamenda Airport past Sacred Heart College into town. First, I made sure there were no soldiers in sight and then I walked on towards town. It was a huge relief to find out that the chaos was further away from the vicinity of my residence. I exchanged greetings with neighbours and other pedestrians as I walked on into town, the heart of the raging altercation. About three weeks already into the State of Emergency, it was now the practice for people to walk the streets gathering the latest information coming in from all over the province, but especially Ntarinkon, Bamenda. This is the neighbourhood where John Fru Ndi, the Chairman of the Social Democratic Front and about 150 others belonging to his party and the party's leadership were still being held under house arrest by Paul Biya's soldiers.

Upon arriving in Ntarinkon, about two kilometres from my house, I encountered the semblance of the reality of what must be going on in the heart of the town. A military truck was speeding in my direction with soldiers tossing tear gas canisters at any group that was along the streets, and so people were running wildly in every direction. I ran in behind a building housing a small shop, Sikadi, as the vehicle roared past—scouts I thought to myself. They were out to see how the other parts of the town were faring so as to plan their own counter attack. If I had any doubts left about the madness and recklessness of the soldiers occupying Bamenda, the speeding vehicle and the behaviour and attitude of the soldiers inside helped me make up my mind with certainty. I had no more doubts I had to keep off the main streets; moreover, my wife's new route ever since the start of the emergency was through the back streets. From Ngomgham, she would walk until Ntarinkon Park, burst in through the park, and then follow the back street towards Hotel Le Bien, but just before the hotel, she would go left through a small marshy area, across a lone stick bridge and then climb up a small slope and into Vicki Street. She would then go left on Vicki Street to Ntamulung Junction across Longla Street, up towards the Longla residence itself, but would turn right onto the street leading to the Bamenda Social Insurance Nursery School. If the times were not too bad, she would then turn right on the street linking Ntamulung from Sonac Street. She would climb up the street onto Sonac Street, turn left on Sonac Street and walk probably half a kilometre to Sendze Building at the Veterinary Junction which was housing *Compagnie Nationale d'Assurance* (CNA), the insurance company for which she worked. Confident of the presence of occupying troops all over Sonac Street, mindful of it being the main artery running through the urban town, it was no news that soldiers would be at every junction along this main street, where crowds could easily form.

I traced my wife's route all the way, but would not go up the Social Insurance Nursery School Street. I instead took the street before that, went past then Government Delegate Pa Abel Tadzong Nde's residence hoping to emerge somewhere below the City Chemist Roundabout and then go left on Sonac Street to my wife's place of work. The noises in the air that came from the City Chemist Roundabout area and Longla Street, as I was soon to find out, did not augur well. There were hundreds and hundreds of young people in the streets taunting a poorly equipped riot unit that dared not venture further on foot out of the safety of the broad and spacious roundabout into the narrow Longla Street where they could easily be ambushed and swallowed up in this human tunnel should another crowd suddenly form behind them. And so from the safety of the roundabout, the soldiers attacked only to retreat immediately back onto the roundabout. The group of soldiers and their behaviour conjured the portrait of a chained dog that can bark and bark as ferociously as possible but cannot charge any further than the length of its chain. This was the brutal and equally bloody dance taking place a street above me when, in my ignorance, I made to emerge from behind the Tanifum residence onto Sonac Street. It landed next to me and made me aware of my surroundings. A huge stone, which no doubt would have cracked my skull and killed me, landed just a few paces in front of me. I looked up suddenly trying to figure out what was happening, only to see a soldier who had stooped to pick up another stone, stretching up to toss it at me. I turned and ran back towards Ntamulung Junction. I was suddenly overwhelmed by fright. The trouble my wife was in had until now been mere speculation; this experience concretized it and made me all the more desperate. I ran all the way back and took the street leading to the Social Insurance Nursery School, hoping my wife had followed that street. I was still running, panting and sweating when in the distance I saw a pink skirt and short-sleeve jacket I thought I recognized headed in my direction. I strained my eyes glaring through my tears and the tear gas that was still in the air; it was my wife. How grateful I was to God; she was smiling, and had a look of surprise when she called out to me even as I jogged on, asking in disbelief where I was headed. She was pleasantly surprised I had taken so much risk, according to her, to come look for her, the mother of our children.

"To find you," I answered. Ita smiled, and in her usually calm and composed manner, declared "Yeah! It is really bad. I don't even know how I made it through."

I hugged her and turned around, and as we walked home, she filled me in on how things had suddenly depreciated into total chaos. My wife made me to understand she had just arrived at her office after about an hour's trek and was trying to settle down when she heard something like singing in the distance coming from the heart of Mankon around the Commercial Avenue. She stepped out of her office to confirm if indeed it was singing she was hearing in the distance. Just then she came face to face with a lot more of what was going on along the streets. A group of young people ran past her office building headed in the direction of Mondial Hotel at the foot of the Station Hill, home to the Government Residential area and the main road meandering out of Bamenda into the neighbouring Western Province.

"Madam, it's bad," shouted a young man as he ran past.

"What's wrong?" Ita called out.

"*Mbélé*" was all she heard as the young man shot past. Then she saw them: heavily armed soldiers jumping off trucks at the Veterinary Junction, cutting off my wife from the residential part of the town. She ran back into her office and bolted the door. A call from her boss, the late Mr. Abongwa Ndita Asangana, may his soul rest in peace, confirmed the fact that she should lock up. Mr. Asangana was telling her he could not pull out of his yard because soldiers were milling all over the place. When he learned that Madam Doh was the only one yet at work, and with soldiers being dropped off all over town, it became obvious there would be no business for the day.

"Lock up Madam, and go home."

"Okay Sir."

"Let's see what Monday would be like."

Ita locked up and sat indoors alone trying to figure out how to get out of her office and go across the road into Ntamulung without clashing with the soldiers. All tensed up and unable to do anything, she sat there waiting and watching through a window for an opportunity to get out of her office and dash across the street into Ntamulung past Ngwena's Off-license on the right and "Awa and Sons" residence on the left, from which neighbourhood she could use back streets all the way home without coming in contact with soldiers.

As the minutes ticked by, she could hear the singing getting louder and louder, confirming her suspicion that the protesters were marching towards Finance Junction where they hoped to join protesters from Nkwen, and together they would all march up station to the Governor's office and deliver their protest; but first they had to march past the soldiers at the Veterinary Junction. According to Ita, there was nothing wrong with the protesters marching, provided they did not destroy property— private or public. The soldiers accordingly, should simply have marched alongside the protesters to ensure there was no destruction, and there would have been no clashes, but typical of a group with little or no crowd control skills, the scene degenerated into one in which the soldiers were determined to prevent the equally determined group from marching to Finance Junction.

The protesters marching to Nkwen were still in front of Progressive Modern Furniture along Sonac Street when all hell broke loose. The men and women in uniform who, hitherto, had been manning the Veterinary Junction, turned and charged in the direction of the approaching protesters with drawn weapons. To Ita, they looked as pathetic as they were chaotic, with the only gist of a strategy being that they took off at once as a group, but there was no formation indicative of organized purpose. And so the soldiers pounced on the protesters striking, punching, and kicking from left to right. As the women in the group of protesters screamed and ran off into the neighbourhoods, the men retaliated with stones and sticks and were able to push back the rag tag squad to their post at the Veterinary Junction before reinforcements arrived. With the arrival of reinforcements, the rioters were forced to retreat, but not before they had erected huge barricades made of the carcasses of vehicles and bulldozers from underneath which weight flames from burning tires soared, leaving the soldiers staring in disbelief. We feared the flames would collide with live wires above and transform the city into an inferno, but it never happened; thank God.

It was during the charge by the soldiers that Ita saw her chance. She snatched her hand bag and rushed out of the office, keyed the lock, and dashed down a flight of stairs in front of her office building and across the street all the way up the slope to the Presbyterian Church at Ntamulung from which advantage point on a knoll she watched the attack and counter attack while catching her breath. Ita knew it was time to go when a soldier from about a hundred feet down below pointed threateningly at her with the baton in his right hand. She was sure they would charge up the hill in her direction if they mistook her for a scout. She ran out of the church's premises into the neighbourhood and found her way to the street from Ntamulung which emerges onto Sonac Street, next to the SONEL (Electricity Corporation) office. She then turned right along the Social Insurance Nursery School street before slowing down to a fast walking pace; it was then she saw me jogging towards her. What a relief it was for both of us. After hugging her, I turned and we walked on, with me listening to what she had been through. Meanwhile, Bamenda was ablaze; one could see thick columns of black smoke rising into the sky from so many different angles with sporadic shouts followed by intermittent attacks by the soldiers who continued firing teargas canisters at the crowd. Then a staccato of machine gun fire would pierce the air leaving us wondering if the soldiers were indeed using live or rubber bullets. There was no way of telling as people scattered in every direction.

It was very embarrassing to see groups of soldiers being led by military captains who were talking from time to time over their radios as if Cameroon was under attack by a foreign nation only for one to realize they were soldiers attacking, beating, maiming, and even killing their own civilians. And nothing has even been done about these excesses, so one is left wondering if these were the orders issued by a thieving, non-patriotic leadership or mere over exuberance by a poorly trained military that has come to equate peace and national stability with the well-being of the dictator in power. Why must a military murder its own citizens and there is never an inquisition into the crime?

My wife and I navigated our way through the back streets, avoiding every major junction where we knew there would be armed soldiers, and got home just before dusk. The kids were very glad to see us, and rushed to welcome their mother. It was almost the end of one more day of Biya's State of Emergency. Even then, the rhythm of civilians being attacked at odd places and equally odd hours in the name of the State of Emergency continued. This notwithstanding, the people of Bamenda were already getting used to the military presence, their harassing behaviour and the rest of their tactics. On one day, all would be calm and quiet, and then just the next morning, the soldiers would work up the population by some stupid strategy of theirs. I remember this morning when a huge military truck with a handful of soldiers was just going around town, and every male about sixteen and above was arrested and thrown into the truck like a sack of cocoyam. The result was that so many people ended up in custody instead of their places of work. How does one account for such provocation? With the people of Bamenda, it is different: revenge! The population decided to ignore the soldiers, denied them food, and got others drunk, resulting in more missing military guns, which, in turn, led to further clashes between the soldiers and the population. I had another first hand encounter on this occasion.

It was about between 5:30 p.m. and many people had returned home from work a little earlier, of course, to avoid the 6:00 p.m. curfew hour. And, as it was now the practice, I was steering my way to the nearest off license in my Ngomgham neighbourhood so as to meet with my neighbours to compare and exchange the latest news of the day. Our spot, a small poorly stocked Off-license, was just across from the Government School at Ngomgham, next to Dr. Formambuh's clinic. We would just sit sipping at our drinks and talking. This is exactly what we were doing this Friday evening, and making plans of walking as far as Ntarinkon around Chairman John Fru Ndi's house for the freshest titbit when, all of a sudden, we heard the roaring and now familiar sound of a speeding truck in the distance. I looked up in the direction of the Bamenda Urban Council building, the only direction from which the vehicle could be approaching—given the direction of the sound— and indeed saw a military truck loaded with armed gendarmes speeding in our direction. It was obvious this was trouble, and there was no point trying to wait and explain ourselves to a bunch of men who had been briefed to teach Bamenda a lesson. And so it did not matter that we were respected members of our community— professors, doctors, lawyers, administrators, traditional elders and the likes.

"Run people, run!" I shouted as I took off. Keeping fit is not a craze in my culture, so rarely does one see an adult running or jogging as they do in other parts of the country. Accordingly, it was with amazement and something like shock, that I noticed my neighbour, Mr. Pius Mbipeh, take off with alarming speed. His height and the speed amounted to a ridiculous and equally laughable blend, but there was not enough time for me to laugh. I was myself speeding as best I could, in a pair of flip-flops, across the Government Primary School field towards Mrs. Bongadu's house which was somewhat en route to mine. With the same glance that caught Mr. Mbipeh showing a clean pair of heels, I caught sight of a gendarme officer speeding after me with his gun gripped firmly across his chest. How wonderful the human mind is; in a split moment, my mind had assessed the situation, and the whole picture before it, and informed me that it would be a disastrous decision if I made a bee line to my house. As a result, I eased my way in the direction of Mrs. Bongadu's house which is lodged across the field and perched on the slope facing Sacred Heart College across on the other hill, not realizing I was running to the targeted spot instead. I later learned that the truckload of gendarmes had been rushed in because they had learned there were plans to burn down Mrs. Bongadu's store and home even. This story was never confirmed, though, given that virtually everything was possible in Bamenda during this period.

As I ran away across the soccer field at Ngomgham Government Primary School, I turned my head to get a last glimpse as to where the gendarmes were headed. Closest to me was a young gendarme officer, but I could tell from his clumsy strides that his rifle, which he grabbed across his chest, was being a hindrance to his effort at catching up with me. His bulging stomach was another encumbrance. I ducked behind a few trees to confuse the officer about my exact destination; in the process, I grabbed the metal fence surrounding my neighbour's building and scaled it. I dashed round his building and jumped over the wall separating my neighbour's yard from mine, and I was home. I immediately went into my house and bolted all my doors just as darkness descended on the valley neighbourhood of Ngomgham where my rented residence was situated. The atmosphere was tense as I explained my experience to my wife, even as we recalled armed soldiers storming into people's homes and harassing them. For the first time, I considered a fenced-in compound a blessing. I have always been against people building beautiful houses and then hemming them in with a fence like that of a maximum security prison, away from the view of would-be admirers. My fence surely held soldiers at bay, coupled with the loud barking of an angry German shepherd and an over-grown Rhodesian ridgeback.

10

We waded through the travails of the State of Emergency, doing all we could to lead normal lives by adapting to the new socio-economic climate, even as the mind struggled with the recent happenings that would leave Bamenda scarred forever.

It was late afternoon the very next day after my close encounter with gendarmes near Ngomgham Government Primary School, and I was sitting in my lounge wondering where the nation was headed when I heard the gunshots echoing off the slope on which my house was lodged. I pulled aside the thick drapes and peeked in the direction from where the shots came. A huge crowd of excited and irate young men had assembled in front of a neighbour's house on the opposite hill—the well-known Alhadji Tita Fomukong. There were all kinds of stories going around about this neighbour especially that which claimed he was a gang boss. I was still trying to figure out what a crowd was doing in front of Alhadji's house when, all of a sudden, Alhadji emerged from his house into the fenced yard in front with a revolver in his right hand, and fired several rounds into the air over the crowd as people dropped to the ground screaming. I wondered where the soldiers were to rescue this man and his family and property if indeed Alhadji was a member of the ruling Cameroon's People Democratic Movement party as it was claimed. Nobody showed up. About thirty minutes had gone by when the overworked police helicopter surfaced from nowhere, it seemed, flew a few circles over the area and apparently half-heartedly tossed several tear gas canisters far away from the angry mob into a nearby valley, to no effect, and then it turned and was gone as quickly as it had showed up.

"We di finish with you today, Alhadji," shouted a young man just as another tossed a flaming tyre onto Alhadji's roof. The tyre would burn for a while, and then the flame would die out. The crowd was undeterred. Several futile efforts were made before another young man shouted out a warning.

"Wuna di waste time. If wuna never cut da mungang for yi waist, da house no fit burn."

Just then, Alhadji made the costly error of stepping out of his house again, possibly to empty a few more rounds above the crowd in the hope of dispelling it when a few daring young men standing close by jumped him. Alhadji ultimately succeeded in running back into his house after struggling with the young men for a while. One claimed to have cut off the charm strapped around Alhadji's waist. Renewed efforts at burning his house down suddenly paid off. A flaming tyre sailed into the building through an open window, just as another lodged itself on the roof of the main building.

Before long, I heard the crowd shouting in jubilation. I rushed out onto my veranda and saw Alhadji's house belching out thick layers of black smoke, even as bright red and blue flames rivalled each other sporadically rising higher and out of the thick smoke. Through a side window, I could tell the fire was growing stronger and stronger by the minute, in spite of the darkness that settled on the valley neighbourhood of Ngomgham. One could hear a woman's cries fading in the distance along with the receding daylight. One was later to learn it was Alhadji's wife who was being carried away half-naked in a wheelbarrow by an angry mob. It was said she had been foul-mouthing Chairman Fru Ndi and the Social Democratic Front Party for sending "vandals" to attack them; the same Fru Ndi who had been held under house arrest by the government. This had offended the crowd more than anything she could have done at that moment.

Nobody knew how terribly wrong things had gone for the Fomukong family until about late morning the next day. Another angry group of young men had stormed Alhadji Fomukong's home early in the morning as if to ascertain the house got burned down indeed. From there they marched angrily down the valley and through a path that emerged right in front of my house. For once, I wondered if my landlord, then with Cameroon's diplomatic service in Washington was a C.P.D.M. member or supporter. I wondered what I would do should these angry young men target the house I was renting. How would I convince them that, because of my belongings, they should spare the building? Just then, the young man at the lead emerged from the path on to the road in front of my compound. Had he turned left, I might have passed out; they went right, and then turned left and up a bushy slope to one of my neighbour's unfinished building. Within a second, the young men were on the roof of the building, and with objects like javelins, pierced hundreds of holes through the zinc roof of the building. The mob was attacking another building when the sounds of the now notorious police helicopter was heard in the distance as it approached Ngomgham, tossing tear gas canisters at the mob. It was another lame effort as the helicopter, once more, went away almost immediately. Just then, word from passers-by gave us to understand that Alhadji Fomukong had died in the fire that ravaged his compound. In fact, his charred body was lying on the floor in the centre of the huge sitting room when I got there. On his torso stood the carefully crafted clay statue of a lion; what bitter humour. The message was clear: he had been killed by Lion Man/*L'homme Lion* as Paul Biya was at the time called because of the use of pictures of a mature lion charging in the open savannah for his election campaign advertisement. According to the pranksters, therefore, Fomukong had been killed by the Lion Man.

One was later to learn that beyond the destruction in my neighbourhood, numerous houses and other personal and public facilities were destroyed. Mr. Ncho's building had been attacked, his expensive and newly installed satellite dish dragged to the ground and destroyed. Unable to burn down his newly completed posh residential building—two stories high—the wiring was short-circuited and destroyed. The most shocking and perhaps the best illustration of the terrible consequences of mob anger and violence, was the destruction of then the latest and equally well built and furnished hotel in town—Bamenda Holiday Resort—which belonged to the same Mr. Ncho, a soft spoken, even humble, one might suggest, business mogul in town. This was a beautiful hotel ideally lodged on an airy slope with an equally beautiful view between Ntsuabuh and the River Mezam. Bamenda was to acknowledge later on that this was a most serious mistake on her part; she had shot herself in the leg by destroying a hotel that was already helping its government-abandoned economy not only to survive but to thrive. One can only imagine then, how this single act negatively affected Bamenda's economic growth. How many indigenes lost their jobs, how much hard currency escaped Bamenda as a result, since tourists could no longer lodge in Bamenda because of the destruction of a modern facility they enjoyed? I hope, and I am convinced, Bamenda will never make such another error blinded as she may be by her justified rage.

Come to think of it, Mr. Ncho was only a lip service C.P.D.M. member we learned. In fact, as usual, word on the grapevine gave us to understand that Mr. Ncho did what he did, went on the air and declared support for the government, albeit in a very weak manner, as a way of causing the government to pay some of the money it owed him since that was the trend. The government under Biya was without standards; it favoured citizens belonging to the ruling party while treating the rest of the citizenry as if they were a foreign burden to a reluctant host government. Alas, Mr. Ncho's declaration was broadcast at the wrong time, however appropriate to the government's cause: to provoke the people of Bamenda to rethink their actions against the government given that a Bamenda business magnate of that calibre was supporting the ruling party and government. With this ostensible "proof" that he was C.P.D.M., virtually every investment belonging to this hardworking indigene was targeted for destruction. It was like piercing one's eyes in order to make a point against a step parent. Mr. Ncho might have recovered from this blow, but not Bamenda. Economically, it was a near suicidal blow by Bamenda to Bamenda in an effort to make a point to a regime that could not care less about this particular part of the country. Under Paul Biya, Bamenda remains incredibly neglected by the government. Herein lies another aberration of the state in Africa.

African governments are the only ones that do not make a secret of the fact that a nation state is a nation state, but an incumbent regime could care less about a part of that so-called nation it is claiming to govern. It is like saying a person abandons his left arm because he writes, eats, and does almost everything with his right hand, and all of this is why most of our leaders are dishonest people. In the case of Cameroon today, the Francophone dominated government could not care less about a buoyant Anglophone minority. They refuse to listen to the complaints of the Anglophones, hoping that in this way the complaints would soon be forgotten, or else resolve themselves. Common sense dictates that procrastination or playing ostrich does not resolve but reschedules the date of a necessary engagement. Sooner or later, the predicament of the Anglophone in Cameroon will be addressed through one means or the other. It may take decades of denial, but like apartheid in South Africa, it will be addressed, or else one day this mirage of a nation will evaporate of its own belligerence. A partner cannot claim to cherish a partner but not listen to his or her complaints about their relationship; that would be sheer hypocrisy, yet this is the case in Cameroon. Whereas Anglophones are complaining, the Francophone dominated regimes, without ever having listened to the Anglophones, deny the fact that Anglophones have a problem. The Anglophones, like civilized people, have always been willing to talk only to meet with Francophone objections, threats, insults, and rejection. But, of course, as history has proven, it takes a genuinely benevolent oppressor to recognize and acknowledge the plight of the oppressed. If the Francophone regimes of Cameroon are not peopled by hypocrites, why then are they refusing to dialogue with the Anglophones about the nature and state of the Union? These tactics by the regimes are only increasing the pressure already existing in this volcano of a nation. Should things continue at this pace, then the result is a question of "when," and not "if" there will be an eruption. Anglophones have no problems with the Francophone population whatsoever. They simply want the Francophone government to recognize their Anglophone colonial heritage from the English, which has become a part of their culture just as it recognizes their Francophone colonial heritage from the French, and is doing all to respect and protect it; that done, they need to be treated like Cameroonians instead of a conquered or colonized people.

That Anglophones are the minority does not accord the hitherto French-backed Francophone majority the right to program their extermination or, at the very least, assimilation. This was the message gradually fed the soldiers occupying Bamenda when there was the opportunity. Late into the second month of the State of Emergency, unfortunately, the soldiers had already developed profound respect for the people of Bamenda instead; they behaved like one person. All efforts to provoke them to attack the heavily armed soldiers so the regime could annihilate the population had failed. Provoked in every humiliating manner possible, the victims and citizens of Bamenda, took it in stoically.

In the oppressive wave institutionalized by Biya's gestapo in Bamenda, Che Ngwa Ghandi was murdered by the soldiers of his own country, supposedly. These are the same men and women who should be protecting Ghandi; this handsome young man, with a beautiful wife and two little daughters at the time. It was rumoured he had been tortured so badly that his organs failed, and then he was dumped at the Bamenda hospital to die—and he died. How does one reconcile oneself to one's country when it brings pain and confusion into one's life? Yes, this is what Paul Biya's Cameroon did to Mrs. Che Ngwa and her children, in particular, and to the people of Bamenda as a whole. The pain doubled and so did the loss of her husband, and the chaos in her family and life when it was found out that Ghandi was not even the rabble-rouser they were looking for, so Ghandi died for nothing. He had lost his life for no reason, simply because some idiot in a position of too much power had made a mistake. True to a chaotic regime like Mr. Biya's, there was no commission of inquiry on the occasion of an innocent Cameroonian's death; it was nothing, but it would have meant something if it were Biya himself who had died, or one of his lackeys sent to torture the people of Bamenda. To Biya, Cameroonians are expendable. After all, remember Nyos, as the disaster which claimed at least a thousand lives came to be known? Until date it is speculated, except for foreign reports, that natural gases escaped from Lake Nyos and decimated everything that breathed for miles around the lake? Did the president ever address the nation? Did he send words of condolence to the people of the North West where this supposed natural disaster occurred? As the people of Cameroon love to put it, "the answer is blowing in the wind" because he did not. It is not surprising then that the president's nonchalance in the face of such a national disaster has led to many other theories about this cataclysm, yet he could not be more indifferent. What then is one Bamenda man's death to this head of state, especially when he was killed by soldiers he sent to teach Bamenda a lesson?

Ghandi's death and the maiming of many brave young men in Bamenda did not matter; their united plight was the bitter lesson, or part of it at least, that the regime wanted Bamenda to learn. After all, they were just a handful; over a thousand had died mysteriously at Nyos, and until today, our beloved president who declared Bamenda his second home is yet to address Bamenda about this natural or artificial massacre. He is yet to address the Cameroon nation about the sudden and equally cataclysmic death of so many Cameroonians. Biya did not even visit the site of this tragic disaster, one of the most blatantly tragic in Cameroon's history. One cannot help wondering if it is Bamenda people, Anglophones, or Cameroonians as a whole, who are expendable to their non-patriotic leaders. At one time it was the Bassas and Bamilekes who were wiped out with French support at the dawn of our independence. Today, however, decades after independence, when Anglophones think they are now living side-by-side with their own brothers and sisters only for this political sibling to turn around and practice what the white man did to us decades before by not only killing Anglophones, but trying to turn them into Francophones.

Three month's heavy military presence and their abuse of power in the way they treated the indigenes, had characterized life in Bamenda from about September 1992 to January 1993 before the powers that be called off their public incarceration of the Bamenda population. The regime must have thought Bamenda would be grateful and not only dance Bikutsi for days in celebration but go down on their knees to thank the president for uplifting the State of Emergency. No, not Bamenda! To this people, a cycle had just been concluded. Barricades went up, flames spurted high into the skies as used tires were piled on barricades across major highways and set ablaze, even as trees were felled and dumped across the roads all over again. The soldiers did not make a move. In groups of three or more, they waited for their exhausted, worn-out looking trucks to pick them up; their drivers having identified different frontage roads that helped them avoid infernal road blocks at major intersections. One could even see soldiers waving from their trucks; they were glad to return home, but above all, they had a newfound respect for a resilient populace that knew when to tell a derailed government enough was enough. Some people smiled back quietly at the waving soldiers, while others waved back. Some of the soldiers were too dazed to wave; they just gave the thumbs up sign as their truck drove past, leaving Bamenda smiling back gently. By night the soldiers were driven out of Bamenda until the last one who had been deployed to Bamenda was gone. But Bamenda had made her point: power belongs to the people. Because their cause was representative of the entire nation, people could not help outwardly displaying their respect for those "graffi" people, even distinguished Francophone politicians and musicians sang their love and respect for Bamenda. It is not surprising the late musician Koto Bass declared about Bamenda in his song "Yes Bamenda," "I no fit forget you," while the rest of the nation could only say in the face of subsequent unpopular government policies "Les gens de Bamenda ne peuvent pas accepter ça," (The people of Bamenda cannot tolerate that).

It was a slow and demanding process for the people's lives to return to normal. Many, now used to trekking to work and buying their daily groceries from the makeshift markets that came into existence in the different neighbourhoods at major intersections, had to go back into the heart of the markets for their needs. As the days came and went, the people of Bamenda, like titans, tended their wounds from their clash with Biya's Gestapo. They had won so many battles, but Biya won the war: he did not relinquish power. Like a real African leader, he clung to office trusting the people would soon forget about the election results and let him go on mismanaging the nation. The nation as a whole let him continue, but the people of Bamenda, Bafoussam, Kumba and Douala especially, have never forgotten the election results of 1992, and the effects it had on the country as a whole. The people of Bamenda and Kumba were tired of fighting against the corrupt regime alone as if the problem of a hijacked Southern Cameroon was mainly theirs; along with Bafoussam and Douala as if the problem of an exploited, derailed, and mismanaged Cameroun was their sole responsibility.

It is almost twenty years since Bamenda's public incarceration in the guise of a State of Emergency, and Cameroon continues spiralling abysmally with once upon a time national symbols—Cameroon Air lines, the Cameroon Development Corporation (CDC), the Water Corporation (SNEC), the Electricity Corporation (SONEL), the oil—being auctioned or mortgaged so that idiotic leaders may continue living in undeserved luxury even as the nation's future is programmed to be dismal. The Douala International Airport, a glorious rendezvous crossroads under Ahmadou Ahidjo is today a wash-house with rain water leaking in all over the place; the streets of Douala along which Cameroonians strolled in the seventies engulfed by national pride as they listened to the latest makossa songs blaring forth from surrounding loudspeakers are today muddy undulations like the exposed muddy belly of a river bed just before a drought; the River Wouri across which meanders the battered Bonaberi bridge which is today a potential source of a national disaster because it can cave in any minute, is a dirty mud bowl with smelly shores where once upon a time idling lovers and sightseers used to take in the view of a busy wharf today deserted by ships in authentication of the nation's economic backwardness and alarming levels of corruption. The roads linking the provinces today, ridiculously referred to as regions as if this change has any significance other than to justify the purposelessness of the Biya regime, are battered here and there, making travelling by road in Cameroon the only venture riskier and more unpredictable than the government's plan for the country. Cameroonians die on a daily basis from avoidable motor accidents, yet the government is still to think it worthwhile figuring out how to prevent this useless loss of Cameroonian lives. Otherwise, how is it that in Cameroon it is okay for a driver driving a huge public transport bus with about seventy passengers to pause at least once during a four hour trip to drink alcohol in the name of "clearing his vision" as they say and the government has no plan in place to deter such suicidal trips and practices endangering the lives of other innocent road users? How can the so-called police force think anything is wrong with this when a uniformed officer on duty along the nation's highway does not think there is anything iniquitous about him brandishing a bottle of beer while in uniform as in groups like vultures they harass travellers in search of bribes claiming to be doing their job, "Je fais mon travail"?

In other parts of the world, as was the case during the Southern Cameroons era and even the West Cameroon days, the embarrassment of the nation's image is considered a serious offence and the culprit, especially if a uniformed officer of the law, pays dearly for it. Not so in Cameroon today; their uniforms are not only dirty, they are torn and of no particular hue as should be the case given that it is a uniform. In addition to this, the officers have no dignity or respectful disposition; they are like thugs using their uniforms to facilitate their thuggery. What a shame! Yes, I have seen members of the uniform corps in Cameroon fighting in the streets with civilians, yet they are called keepers of the peace and paid with the tax payer's money. Accordingly, one cannot help but wonder what their curriculum in the Police College or Military Academy is all about, yet that is Cameroon.

11

The years have come and gone with Cameroonians in disbelief that Biya "joked" like this and clung to power. One is left with a feeling of emptiness akin to that experienced by the North West Province, in fact the whole of Anglophone Cameroon, in 1979, when their darling football team, PWD Bamenda climbed to a high point such that it was an authority in Cameroonian football. They were to play the finals of the Cameroon nation's cup against Dynamo, Douala, and virtually everyone was sure Bamenda was going to win that cup that year. Alas, a traitor was to emerge from within Bamenda's ranks and betray the squad by intentionally facilitating goals against his own team, or something to that effect. That was probably the first time the rage of Bamenda people was displayed in the open in recent years. Epese, as the traitor was called, was smart enough not to return to Bamenda with the team; it would have meant his life. His property was emptied from the house he was renting and burnt and his girlfriend had to run and hide for her life. Until date, the name Epese in Bamenda is synonymous to "traitor," and the people use it in this manner all the time. From time to time, this use of the name gives them an opportunity to re-live their victory of a nation's cup they never won, and then slowly you will see people moving away and shaking their heads in disbelief. This is still the reaction in Bamenda today whenever the presidential election results of 1992 are discussed. It was not a Bamenda thing but a national disaster. The entire nation was fed up and wanted change;

they came this close to it but failed to pool their resources together as one people to claim their stolen victory. They left the responsibility mainly in the hands of four daring cities, with Bamenda spearheading the way. Had the entire nation, even without the Bikutsi base of the president run amok, the story would have been different today as the dilapidated government machinery would not have been able to handle the pressure. When a people stand together as one person and say "no," there is nothing any government can do.

After all the hoopla, with dead and limbless patriots in the wake of this political statement, through the grapevine, one hears that Fru Ndi and Biya are pals; that they even eat together. It is said Fru Ndi, once thought of as the Messiah for the struggling masses of Cameroon sucks on a pacifier plopped into his mouth by the man against whom we all once struggled, and made incredible sacrifices so there could be change some day. Today, Fru Ndi, it is said, cruises around in a luxurious SUV cut off from the suffering masses by tinted windows; the man for whom Bamenda, especially, was ready to cease existing. He has overgrown his house at Ntarinkon and so only drives through town basking in the quickly fading image of himself, when compared to the nineties, as Cameroon's only trusted presidential candidate. Of his agenda, hardly much else is known other than that, as rumoured, he shuttles from his huge farm in Fundong to another in Yaounde. But rumours, rumours have a way of tainting one, especially a man like Chairman John Fru Ndi. Had I not been in Bamenda and different venues and seen Fru Ndi put his life on the line, I would have fallen for these stories, yet the stories are still making rounds leaving most of us wondering what is going on, if Pa himself has eaten *suya*?

In which case we were all pawns used for his socio-political aspirations, thinking he loved and cared for the suffering masses. Even as I fight against this new portrait some are painting of our hero, the truth is that I doubt if Mr. Fru Ndi has any plans for those brave young men who lost their limbs pushing his and our political agenda forward. I used to see them, today reduced to beggars because of their handicap. They are begging from bus to bus at different transport agencies such as Guarantee, Amour Mezam and so on, from passengers with whom they once dared to dream of a better Cameroon. We give them mites from time to time because we remember these heroes by whom we once waded in an atmosphere shrouded by waves of tear gas clouds even as our sons and daughters in uniforms trained guns at us, took aim, and fired. Many dropped with gaping wounds ripped open by bullets, yet today while our once upon-a-time rebel leader cruises along basking in his well-deserved fame, I worry that he might have forgotten these casualties, these true heroes whom I fear, in the quiet solitary moments of their current lives, wonder what it was all about and if it was worth it. Had Mohandas Karamchand Ghandi gone back to wearing suits, what would his struggle have been about? Something must be done for these real heroes of ours; it is the least the nation owes them. Unfortunately, ours is far from being that kind of a nation to which its citizens mean everything. Ours is a nation to which the priority is the welfare and maintenance of power by the dictator in office. Every other citizen is of little or no consequence, and so the masses continue to chaff, portrayed as beggars, the wretched of God's fertile earth while cliques, societies, sects, cabals, and brotherhoods mismanage our nation which ought to have been a paradise given our resources and the scanty national population. Even then, the ruling banditti continues squeezing the working masses dry of every financial drop they try to come up with for their families to survive on. Else why are there toll gates along Cameroon's roads today? What do they do with the money when the very roads along which toll is collected contradict the essence of the whole exercise with huge, frightening potholes and blind corners that all amount to a recipe for ghastly accidents which are never out of season? Simon Achidi Achu's gift to his people for all his years as a privileged member of the "eating class" from as far back as the Ahidjo era until of recent; another purposeless tax squeezed out of an already over taxed yet poorly served citizenry.

Accordingly, like a true Southern Cameroonian, each time I look back at where I came from as a citizen, I am left wondering even as my own life begins its descent into the grave, what the future is going to be like for our children. As a people we have been nomads coming and going—with this or that name—according to the political whims and caprices of those wielding power, unfortunately, to whom we are mere ragdolls and baits as the seasons come and go. I was not there when we were one people under the Germans, Kamerun. However, when I could talk, read and write, I saw a few signboards with "Kamerun" on them, but I read documents with our people referred to as Southern Cameroonians. I can remember the order that existed in our society even as the problems with the U.P.C. in French Cameroon escalated, causing some party members to escape into West Cameroons. By this time, the Germans had been defeated in World War 1 and so her African territories, Kamerun being one, were partitioned and handed over to the allied forces as war booty, in my opinion, even though western historians would love the world to believe these regions were just protectorates to be aided through the process of self-administration, like toddlers, until they could stand on their own. If this were the case, Kamerun could simply have been handed over whole to France or to Britain. But the balance of power and interests in Africa and around the world as a whole on the part of the west had to be maintained. And so, even with the northern part of Nigeria which was part of Southern Cameroon, the smaller part of Kamerun went to Britain, and the larger to France. In this way, a people are transformed into cultural aliens later on unable to recognize themselves, let alone coexist; it is not surprising then that the majority Francophone population cannot stomach the Anglophone minority.

In the union that emerged, the Federal Republic of Cameroon, the truth is that Francophones, Kamerunians who found themselves under France, came in with a hidden agenda. They had been dishonest from the onset. Both parts of Kamerun had now acquired different colonial cultures, and so were now different peoples given the trends of westernized governing methods they had acquired. It was agreed then, that a federation in which these different colonial cultures would be respected was the kind of union into which both factions would come. Accordingly, English-speaking Cameroon was called West Cameroon, and French-speaking Cameroon, East Cameroon. Indeed our systems were different—education, the judiciary, security, and so on. The dishonesty of Francophone politicians comes to the fore when it is realized that slowly but surely Ahidjo built and set in place a Gestapo, answerable to him alone, which he used in eliminating his rivals and opponents, even as he distorted the structure of the federation Cameroon was supposed to be. He weakened the once stronger socio-economic structure of West Cameroon and made her dependent on federal resources over which he was totally in control. The hidden agenda was to slowly eliminate the Anglophone culture completely. To those Francophones who have seen the strengths of the Anglophone system of education such that they write in English as if they are Anglophones, their goal being to confuse the younger generation of Anglophones since they write in English causing a cloud of confusion over the Anglophone cause, is this fair? If the Francophone majority can respect the French culture they acquired during colonialism, why do they think it is all right for them to force Anglophones to abandon the English values they assimilated which remain superior in many ways? This dishonesty is the backbone of Cameroon's problems between the former East and West Cameroon. Within the East, there are ethnic tensions, mindful of the fact that the Bassas and the Bamilekes are yet to forget what the French-backed Ahidjo regime did to them, but these intra-state conflicts must not be confused with the interstate, that is the Federal problem between the states of East and West Cameroon. The Bassa or Bamileke problem cannot then be put at par with the Anglophone problem as certain detractors are trying to do. To attempt doing this is not only malicious but amounts to a betrayal of gross ignorance about Cameroon's history, which will not be that surprising in any case given that most of our own were brought up studying mainly European instead of African history.

Accordingly, Anglophone nationality has gone from Southern Cameroonian to West Cameroonian, to Cameroonian under the United Republic of Cameroon and finally to Anglophone-Cameroonian (albeit against what the government would like it to be) under the travesty of a nation today called the Republic of Cameroon. English speaking Cameroonians have never been part of the Republic of Cameroon. When the Republic of Cameroon (La République du Cameroun) was in existence, English speaking Cameroonians belonged to a community called Southern Cameroons, different from the Federal Republic of Nigeria from which nation's capital, Lagos, at the time, Southern Cameroonians were being indirectly administered by Britain. Southern Cameroonians gained their independence (if this could honestly be called gaining one's independence) by joining La République in a federated state—the Federal Republic of Cameroon. By calling the nation today simply the Republic of Cameroon, just because the Francophones are the majority, has led to a miscarriage of the terms that kept us as a nation. In other words, La République has opted out of the union be it a Federal or a United Republic. This is the problem in Cameroon today, and then to make things worse, Anglophones are being treated as beggars, outsiders in their own geographical space. We have called for a national conference to discuss this very important issue which has to do with the nation's stability and growth only for Francophone-dominated regimes to keep rejecting the invitation.

We all know from history that it takes a lot more from the oppressed to help the oppressor to acknowledge the former's plight of which he is aware but is always reluctant to admit, especially in public, since he is the beneficiary from the status quo. And so, the struggle continues, even as we search for a befitting national nomenclature for our people. Even then, history shall pass judgement on Anglophones, especially those individuals and groups that have betrayed the Southern Cameroons cause for shameful titbits, personal or communal. We are a people, grouped together by history, and so together we must uphold our course despite misguided and irrelevant arguments about cultural similarities and dissimilarities and so on. The human body remains the united whole that it is, the differences between the limbs and the torso notwithstanding. In like manner, the overwhelming similarity between human beings and apes has never made the former to feel like strongly identifying with the latter.

I continue to cry for the days of Southern Cameroons, even West Cameroon, when there was peace, love, respect and hard work. I realize I am not alone. Ephraim Ngwafor continues to dream that, albeit as a microcosm, former Victoria may smile again. To forget who we are as a people is to lose our identity, and to lose one's identity is to become an object; we know better. Our past must be revisited and our future looked into for us to belong. If La République hungers to see herself as she was before, such that she has reverted to her old name La République du Cameroun, so do we, Southern Cameroonians. Otherwise, we must all make that sacrifice by standing together—Francophones and Anglophones—and in all honesty work towards building a Cameroon that belongs to and acknowledges all her children instead of these treasonable approaches at governance and so-called nation-building now thriving.

www.ingramcontent.com/pod-product-compliance
Lightning Source LLC
Chambersburg PA
CBHW011713290426
44113CB00019B/2664